## Self-Publishing: Absolute Beginners Guide

| | |
|---|---|
| Foreword | 4 |
| Introduction Imogene Nix | 5 |
| Introduction Suzi Love | 8 |
| Time To Write | 10 |
| Self-Editing | 15 |
| There's More | 24 |
| Self-Publishing Is Different | 27 |
| Cover Art | 33 |
| Imogene's Final Words | 42 |
| What's Next? | 43 |
| Self-Publishing Nitty-Gritty | 57 |
| Getting Your Book Ready | 62 |
| Selling Your Book | 73 |
| Copyright | 84 |
| Formatting | 89 |
| Suzi's Final Words | 97 |
| Cheat Sheets and Your Notes | 105 |
| Checklists For Self-Publishing | 108 |
| About Imogene Nix | 112 |
| About Suzi Love | 115 |
| Afterword | 116 |
| Notes | 117 |

Self-Publishing: Absolute Beginners Guide

Copyright © 2016 by Imogene Nix and Suzi Love

With An Additional Formatting Guide
By Copyright @2016 Sassie Lewis

ISBN Print - 9780994502315
ISBN eBook - 9780994502322

All rights reserved.
No part of this book may be reproduced
in any form or by any electronic
or mechanical means, including information
storage and retrieval systems,
without written permission from the authors,
except for the use of brief quotations
in a book review.

N.B. This book uses British English.

**SELF-PUBLISHING:**

**ABSOLUTE BEGINNERS GUIDE**

# *Foreword*

### Self-Publishing - Absolute Beginners Guide

Information, advice, and tips to help you decide between Self-Publishing or Traditional Publishing, and to then get you started on your road to publication.

This detailed information gives contacts, lists, cheat sheets, and checklists that can be reproduced over and over again, helping set goals that will steer you towards professionally produced books.

The book is aimed at all authors, fiction and non-fiction, and is available in a range of formats including digital and paperback.

Co-Authored by two Australians, multi-published Imogene Nix and best-selling and award winning Suzi Love.

To learn more about us and our new releases, join our newsletters at Imogene Nix and Suzi Love.

# *Introduction Imogene Nix*

### New authors think the writing part of the job is the hardest.

If only this were true. The writing part certainly takes time and skill, but it's merely the tip of the iceberg when it comes to writing. My name is Imogene Nix and I'm an author. I can say that now, with over 25 books to my name, 6 completed series and a range of self-published titles. Like a lot of new authors, I dove into the publishing world the "oh once I've written my book, that's the end of the hard work," at the forefront of my mind.

Sadly, the day of submitting, receiving a contract and letting the publisher do most of the marketing work has passed. In today's rapidly changing world of authorship, what sets an author apart, and makes them a success, is the effort and professionalism of their work. As you would be aware, the world of publishing is changing at an extraordinary pace, sweeping along the tide of self-publishing with it.

However, just today, I read an article that had impact. The author wrote that only 40 authors had "made it" with self-publishing in the last 5 years. Only 40. Now, to be fair, they were saying that "made it," meant earning $1 million or more in that time. But it's still sobering to hear these figures.

The grim reality is 99% of all authors will not earn enough to live on. Of those, many will not earn back the costs of self-publishing on their titles, but for those who can make a profit, chances are, they're more than good writers. They must be publicists, authors, editors, blog gurus and a whole heap more besides! When you look at it like that, it's enough to make you step back and wonder why you want to do that.

One of the questions I'm regularly asked is "what is the best piece of advice you could give new authors?" I always answer, work out what you want to be. Will you be an author or a writer? They have completely different perspectives and desired outcomes.

An author is a professional, seeking to make a living from the creative role they fulfill. A writer can do so for fun, for money and to see their name in print. So I'll ask you the same question. What do you want to be?

With this in mind, we can proceed to considering your story or book and making decisions about what you want to do with it. The publishing game is difficult, riddled with opportunities to make mistakes, and some of them will mean big $$, while others will result in lost sales and some even a loss of face. Take heart though, because there are options. Lots of them and you can survive the murky waters of publishing - not to just survive, but to maybe produce the next Best Seller. And that's what we're in this game for, isn't it?

### **Success is made up of energy, persistence, talent and timing!**

In fact, I'd liken writing a book to baking a cake. There is a recipe (yes, others wouldn't agree) but the concept is the same. Your recipe differs from flavour to flavour and it's no different with a book! Sometimes it's simple, you just throw the ingredients into the bowl, mix, pour into a tray and bake. Other times, it's weigh, measure, and only stir one way... You get the idea, I hope.

I'm a firm believer in weighing, measuring and baking carefully when writing. Keeping to the recipe is why I've got a range of books with differing publishers. It's why several of my books have Best Seller tags on them. It's why my friend and co-author Suzi is also a Best Seller in her genre.

You too can achieve these outcomes. All it takes is imagination, time and creativity. Let's be brutally honest for a moment, with something in the region of 3, 000 books published monthly on Amazon alone, it's going to take effort to get noticed, but it can be done.

This book is not an exhaustive guide, nor is it a step-by-step how to for creating and marketing your book. It's simply the things we've learned along the way. I use examples of how to and how not to do things, tips to help you avoid the pitfalls so many authors stumble into when they first start out and our honest opinions based on our experiences.

I wish you the best of luck with your writing career. It's exciting and exacting but never dull!

*Introduction by Imogene Nix*

# *Introduction Suzi Love*

My name is Suzi and I'm also an author.

I love saying that! Though it took several years and a lot of hard work before I became a published author.

Self-publishing allows you to sell your book in print, digital and market directly to readers. You become an entrepreneur, rather than an author, and are in control of every phase.

But be warned, self-publishing is not a get-rich-quick scheme, nor is it a place to sell substandard books. The huge influx of sub-standard books self-published about 2-3 years ago gave all self-publishing authors a bad name, and readers, book bloggers, etc. are very discerning.

When you self-publish, you are responsible for organising all the following - editing and proofreading, cover art, writing teaser or back cover copy (back cover blurb), writing your author bio, final layout and production of the physical book or digital book files, adding excerpts from your other books into the back, purchasing an ISBN, setting prices, arranging promotion, requesting quotes from big-name authors (optional) and sending out copies for review (optional).

So you should weigh up the pros and cons for you before you start and decide if it definitely what you want and if you will be able to do all the work. Some of the reason why authors decide to self-publish include – A book isn't right for traditional publishers and/or has a specific niche market where you can sell it better by yourself.

You're the sort of author who doesn't like handing over control unless you can be certain that a publishing house can do a better job of retailing your book than you can. Or you don't like the terms of the publishing contracts being offered, as they might lock in your book for anywhere from two to ten years, and sometimes forever.

Or you'd like to know your daily sales figures rather than waiting to be paid royalties, which might only be every three or even six months. Perhaps you'd like to earn 70% royalties rather than 25-30%, because that money is always better in your pocket than someone else's. And one of main reasons authors self-publish books is if they have had book rights reverted from a publisher due to a contract finishing or perhaps a publisher closing.

Before making the decision to Self-Publish, you should ask yourself some of these questions.

Do you have a business plan or have you made a yearly writing plan?

Have you ever run your own business before?

Will you write under your legal name, pseudonym, or publishing company or, if using your real name, are you able to ensure your privacy and safety won't become an issue, especially if you are writing hotter books?

Are you aiming for digital alone, or will you be doing print, audio, and/ or foreign translations in the future?

How many books do you plan to publish and will book sales be your primary income from the start, or later?

Do you already have a readership already or will you need to build sales from the ground up?

Do you have enough money set aside to pay for outsourcing jobs such as a cover artist, an editor, a proofreader, promotion sites?

And lastly, how much do you already know about self-publishing and how much do you need to learn before you can start self-publishing books and earning some income?

*Introduction by Suzi Love*

## *Time To Write*

It's time to write. You've got the urge and you're ready to carve time from your busy schedule. That's fabulous! You've taken the first step in creating a story that's engaging and well written.

This is as good a place to start. When it comes to the world of writing, you're going to hear all sorts of terms related to writing. They'll talk about computer word counts, pantstering and plotting and so on, but what does all that mean? Let's deal with some of the more common phrases you'll come across.

### Pantster Vs Plotting or somewhere in between with Imogene

I'm a pantster. I like to write by the seat of my pants and have very little knowledge of what's going to happen before I sit down to write. There's nothing wrong with that at all. In fact, I enjoy it. A lot of authors will tell you though, that it isn't a proper method of writing. Here's how I work: I set aside time each day and write until my story is done. I have a rough idea in my head and let it tumble out word by word.

Plotters use a range of post-it note, diagrammatical charts and other devices to forward plan every step, interaction and activity. Flash cards, scene cards and even sketches! For me, that feels contrived and creates a stilted sense of the story.

The important thing to remember here, is everyone formulates their own pattern of writing. If you feel you need a blackboard, power point presentation, etc., great! Just remember, as a writer & aspiring author, you are the one that sets your own standard.

Don't let anyone bully you and say there is only one way. That's not true.

**Word Count:** You will hear this a lot when it gets to the brass tacks of writing. It's simply the amount of words in your manuscript. If you use any older "how to" manuals, they will talk about the algorithm for working out your word count. In most instances, don't worry about it. It's an anachronism. These days, unless asked for, all you need is the computer word count — that is, whatever the count on the bottom of your computer screen tells you once you turn in the completed manuscript.

**Microsoft Word:** Love it or hate it, most editors, publishers and published authors use word because it allows files to be saved in the RTF (Rich Text File) format used by publishing houses.

**Manuscript:** This is the raw, completed version of the story. It can be edited or unedited.

**Editors:** While I cover editing in more detail in this book, in essence, an editor polishes your story to help it shine.

**Cover Artists:** Cover Artists are the people who create the cover art, ensuring that they adhere to Copyright restrictions with their use of images, that they meet the criteria of size and definition required for all sites.

**Agents:** Agents are people who can act for an on behalf of authors. Most self-publishing authors do not have them, as a self-publisher is in direct control of all aspects of the publishing process. They can also be very hard to obtain and frequently charge a percentage of the total royalty received by authors. This fee system is included in the contract entered into by both author and agent. Publishers are not party to this contract.

**Submitting**: The act of sending a manuscript to a publisher or agent for the purposes of obtaining a publishing contract.

**Submission Guidelines**: The rules of submission as laid down by a publishing house. If you choose to submit your title to a publisher, ensure you check these carefully as they govern everything from content, to submission process and layout of the manuscript. Should you choose to go down this path, ensure you adhere to their guidelines.

**Copyright**: Copyright is the exclusive and assignable legal right, given to the originator for a fixed number of years, to print, publish, perform, film, or record literary, artistic, or musical material.

**Legal Deposit**: In Australia, any book that is published must have a copy lodged with the National Library of Australia. This is called Legal Deposit. For full details, visit the National Library website. www.nla.gov.au

## How long, How much, When, Where & Why with Imogene

Depending on what kind of writer you've determined you are, it helps to have a guideline to the following questions: How long will your story be?

For sure, if you're a pantster you may not have the accurate number to the nearest hundred words, but usually by the time you hit around the first ten thousand words, you'll have an idea how long the story will run for. After all, your story has a number of discrete things that must happen.

There must be a problem, there must be a plan for addressing the problem, and you must conclude/defeat the problem.

Books come in a range of lengths, including Novellas, Novels and so on. I tend to write either novellas - about the 30,000 – 40,000 word length and novels 50,000 – 85,000 word length.

Individual publishers have their own guidelines for story lengths. Once you've determined your target publisher (or if you're self-publishing) you need to find out what is the usual length for your story. In self-publishing, it's not such a big deal, but there are loose guidelines here too.

Are you writing a Science Fiction/Urban Fantasy/Romance/Crime & Suspense title? It helps to be a reader of the genre so you can gauge what are the usual devices used in those kinds of stories.

What time frame are you working with? If you're writing historical, it is strongly recommended that you engage in your research as early as possible.

## A Note on stories incorporating FACTUAL information:

Depending on what kind of story you are writing ENSURE that if there is factual (scientific or historical) information to be used, that you adequately research it.

I write science fiction and tend to get caught up in the need to research. Because I write and write and write, I have no idea what kind of research I may need to do before I begin. I have found that when I hit a point that is scientifically driven, I must stop and research immediately when I get to that point.

Research though is not a mere check of Wikipedia. If you plan to use accurate detail (and trust me your readers WILL call you on it if you get it wrong!), you need to ensure your data gathering is rigorous and accurate.

Nothing will bring your book down, quite so quickly, as being called a fraud for inaccurate historical/scientific information.

If, for instance you write a Victorian romance novel, you need to know what kind of underwear was used at that time. There's no use inserting panties instead of bloomers or pantaloons. Readers can, and will, pick up on that.

Also, AK47's were not around in the time of Emperor Nero—unless you have a time travelling bad guy, that is! These inaccuracies stick out like a sore thumb :)

Lastly, I would strongly suggest you work out WHY you want to be published. Is it to be able to say you have a book printed? This can and will affect what options you may consider down the track when it comes to producing copies of your books.

If you're in it for commercial purposes, then your book needs to be bigger, better and more desirable then Joe Bloggs down the street who is only doing it for Mum and Aunty Pam.

It needs to be professionally edited, and you need to consider distribution channels... marketing plans...

# *Self-Editing*

This is where I caution you to put your work aside and let it settle in your mind. I prescribe nothing less than one month's break. This allows you to clear the preconceptions you've gathered before returning to your work.

### **Why?**

When you write a book, your fingers move to the beat of the story in your head. Because you work at a rapid pace, there is a chance that you could miss words, spell things incorrectly. When you go back with the preconception, your mind thinks that you've got the right word or spelling. You need a break to clear it from your psyche long enough that it's had time to reset.

Now, self-editing can be done a range of ways. The best one I've seen, is to read the words out loud as you check. It can be embarrassing. It can be confronting. It works. Sitting in a darkened room, trying to read a sex scene out loud. Try that and not blush. Even after 20+ books. Some people use the speaking facility in their word processing package and find it picks up all kinds of interesting things, such as typos and grammatical mistakes.

However you do it, it encourages your brain to consider your writing in another way and highlights mistakes your brain misses, because it focuses on what it thinks you've written!

Remember, when you're self-editing, this is the time to pick up on anything from missing full stops to ellipses. If you don't have any experience with self-editing, I strongly recommend you invest in a book that deals with that, perhaps something along the lines of Eats, Shoots & Leaves. (I'll include the biographical data at the end of this book.)

There are lots of good books out there, so find one that works for you. Also, many publishers have their own individual style guides. If you intend to submit to a specific house or find one you like, download it and refer back.

During this editing phase is also a good time to expand on missing information, to answer questions concerning the story and simply flesh out my title. Once satisfied, I send it off to my Beta Reader for their initial read through. (They will often see it twice or more times!)

### Is it time yet to Edit with Imogene?

No! Or at least not in the traditional sense that most without publishing experience would think. Why? Because that step comes later. Much, much later!

Between now and edits, is a good time to re-edit based on the feedback you've received from your Beta Reader. Make sure to think long and hard, because in many instances, this is it. The penultimate point of pre-submission.

### TIP! Before I go any further, let me state for the records...

An editor is NOT your high school English teacher.

This is not meant to be argument inducing. The truth is editing is a very specific set of tools, and authors must adhere to a range of techniques that are not commonplace in an English classroom.

The art of editing a professional title is not their role. (That is, unless they are trained for it.) I polled writers and editors to come up with the following points... (This list is NOT comprehensive, but a starting point...)

- E.g.

- Editors say no adverbs, yet English teachers love them. (lively, jovially etc.)

- Semi colons are verboten in manuscripts. (;)

- English teachers would discourage the em dash in favour of the semi colon

- English teachers don't mind continuous past tense... (was walking) Editors demand simple past... (walked)

- English teachers adore varied dialogue tags. Editors want it simple - (English Teacher - He instructed) (Editor - He said) ... that is if you are allowed to use a dialogue tag.

- If doing a developmental edit, the editor decides if the whole story hangs together. Characterization, dialogue, etc.

- English teachers don't mind omniscient, objective third person. Editors want deep, subjective point of view.

**<u>A final word from a teacher (30 year's experience) who happens to be a trained editor (10 year's experience).</u>**

An English teacher usually works with kids who are in the process of developing their control of language. She/he should encourage experimentation and exploring the places language can go. Whether or not that would be popular or marketable is irrelevant.

An editor should be working with someone who has already mastered the language and needs, instead, an objective opinion of what is needed to make the work clear, succinct and both appealing to readers and marketable.

An editor should also be more concerned to make sure the work fits into current guidelines and recommendations, where a teacher will be more concerned with the student undergoing a learning experience, where the end result is not as important as the skills learned. With that out of the way let's go directly to the mixing of your cake... your book.

In order to find the right balance you need two things.

- At least one GOOD critique partner
- At least one QUALITY Beta Reader

As a professional author, I'm going to give you a piece of advice. DO NOT ask your best friend, your mum or Aunty Beryl to fill these positions. You know that their feedback, will, most likely be, how clever, brilliant, awesome you are. (While that's nice... it's not USEFUL feedback.) You need someone who will be honest. Now that's not to say you can't show them, but I have found the feedback you get is, "That's brilliant! You are so clever." You need someone who is prepared to tell you when aspects just don't work. You need someone who can make educated suggestions about your work.

### The same with a Beta Reader.

Now, it's not easy to find them. You need someone you can trust. Someone you feel comfortable with, but who won't be afraid to tell you the hard stuff. The "you've written garbage..." stuff. A lot will never be honest enough to feel they can say that.

Sadly, in the world of writing, you need someone with the chops to be brutally honest and to call you on padding (filling pages with useless, go nowhere content) and other unnecessary detritus. I have two exceptional Beta Readers. They have been known to send me back pages and pages of questions. That's good, because these are the questions your editors and readers will ask.

### TIP!

Your beta reader and critique partner do not have to be authors, but it helps! They will give you feedback, but at the end of the day, it's your decision whether to accept or not what they suggest.

One last word...

Not all critique partners /beta readers stick with you forever. If it doesn't work... It doesn't. Don't give up. Get out there and look again. Eventually you will find a core group who will help you be the best author you can be.

### Critique? Beta? I'm Lost with Imogene

Critique partners are special. They can enhance your story or destroy your morale. There are written and unwritten rules in this area. It's always wise to approach this with a set of guidelines so everyone agrees on the desired outcomes.

Here are some handy starting points you can give to your critique partner, so you all know how to begin.

### Hostess Gifts are always welcome.

As with most things, when you turn up to a party, preparation is the key. In the world of writing that means really giving the piece you are looking at consideration.

Note making (and I really love the handy "Track Changes" tab in Word for this) means you can make notations and corrections, allowing the person you are reading for, feedback at the point of the writing, rather than asking the author to hunt and pick the information you mention.

### Being Kind

Sadly, we've all seen reviews where the reader attacks the author, calling them all kinds of things. With critiquing the key is to focus on the piece.

Remember it's your job to point out what you think are issues with the work, consider how you word any perceived issues so it blunts the trauma of delivery.

### **Lead With A Positive**

It's really easy to start out focusing on the negative, but every story or book has a positive, so I always recommend starting with that. An author will be far more open and receptive to your corrections when they see that the piece they've slaved over has been carefully considered and the positives treated with the same level of interest as the negatives.

### **Read For Enjoyment**

Okay, so you've read a book and honestly, in your mind, it isn't worth the paper it's written on. Ouch! Wording like that really turns off an author and could potentially put your friendship at risk.

If you honestly feel you can't find a positive, the first and most important thing you can do is to decline the critique. So you don't like the fact they've written about vampires or a young girl in a forest wearing a scarlet coat...

Remember, at the end of the day, this story was crafted for someone's enjoyment. It might be that you aren't the target audience. Try and get into the story though, give it a chance. Who knows, it may just appeal to you.

### **Getting It Right**

So you've given the positives, approached it in a professional manner... Great! Now comes the hard bit, telling it as it is. A lot of times, the feedback given to an author, when focusing on short comings tends to be, "this is the same word for the 50 000th time," or "can you come up with another word because this doesn't make sense to me."

Above all, use constructive language, such as "This might be better with XXX word," "Perhaps a stronger word might be xxx," or "if you change this to XX it might be a more exciting way to describe it."

Your author has asked for and appreciates your feedback, so in order to help them improve their writing, make suggestions, think about how you approach weaknesses and above all enjoy your role.

## Tips for the Author

## After The Storm

Okay, you have the critique back and the sea of red seems downright overwhelming. Remember all authors have been down this road before. Yes, it's hard to open the file and take it as a positive step forward, but honestly, this is just another step on the road to authorship. You may even feel like it's not worth continuing.

When you take the step of asking someone to critique your work, it isn't about you. It's about strengthening your writing. Of course, you won't agree with everything they say. How could you?

The important thing to remember is that they have taken the time to read your manuscript, to work out the dynamics of the characters and so on.

When you are ready, most authors need a Beta Reader. What do they do? They are NOT your critique partners. They are readers who will take your story, ask lots of questions. Point out plot holes and bits they don't understand.

This is a valuable and important part of authorship. It can be hard. Even confronting. Particularly if they don't like the story. But what it will do, is give you valuable feedback from readers.

## So Tell Me About Beta Readers.

One really good Beta Reader is worth a dozen of so-so ones. Why? Because it's their work that will make you think about the story, the twists and turns. The mechanical details of what makes it flow. They are the ones who will read your story and tell you, realistically, if it made sense or a load of codswallop.

Sure, it's likely your critique partner has already done that, but think of a Beta Reader as your last line of defence. Finding one isn't easy. As with a critique partner, you need someone who won't pull punches. Someone who will tell you the unvarnished truth.

Look around for someone who reads in your genre, because they are your TARGET AUDIENCE, the ones who will buy your book. The ones that will be your harshest critics.

In order to be sure that you cover as many bases. You aren't going to give an Erotica reader a Young Adult title. You aren't going to give a mechanic a recipe book. Think about the age, experience, interests of your reader and actively find someone who reads or is of that age, gender, etc.

Don't have someone you can ask? Seek out someone with publishing experience. Someone who already knows the ropes. It won't be an ideal fit, but at least they will be able to look at it from the point of view of someone who might know how to ask the right questions.

You need someone who can tell you the truth, but knows how to be kind in the delivery. This isn't about destroying your hopes and dreams, but someone who will question what you've written, urge you to dig deeper and challenge you to prove your research. Criticism is welcome so long as it's balanced!

Be careful that they don't read your manuscript more than say, once or twice. Anything more than that and they become invested in your story, or book. While you want them to feel that they've assisted you, it's easy to fall into the trap where they, like you, aren't able to look at it objectively.

If you belong to a writers group, you might find an ideal candidate there! Other writers understand the tyranny of writing. They can be objective (usually) and many have already been there. If you decide to go down that track, be very sure that they understand they are Beta'ing and not critiquing. Yes, it's a subtlety, but important to ensure they know what you want from them.

But if you really want to know more about this, a quick Google search will show you lots of how to's that deal with this issue in depth. We would suggest that you take some time and learn the tricks and tips of the trade before you proceed further.

# *There's More*

### But Wait! There's more!

Before your book is ready for submission, you need to edit your work AGAIN. Find out what information is useful and what isn't. Read through what your Beta reader and Critique partner point out. As an author, you need to determine what suggestions will improve your story – make it better but still yours... versus someone else's work. Sometimes it can be daunting. I hate opening the emails I get back once they return. The sea of red (and it always feels like that, even after 20+ books) can be hard to deal with.

I suggest open, read then close down. Take a break. Take your time. See whether you feel that connection in their corrections and comments. Do the suggestions make sense? Do they sound like you? If they don't then be cautious. That's not to say, you shouldn't consider these points, but ensure that they don't overwhelm your work. Whatever you decide (and this is an intensely person part of the job) weigh up whether your work will benefit.

### Rule of thumb: If in doubt, throw it out!

Prepare yourself before you begin, then settle in and work thought every comment - whether you accept/decline is your choice, but make sure everything is addressed.

### TIP!

Every writer has a "voice" ... This is the thing that makes your writing distinctive. It could be that you use a lot of humour. It could be syntax.

Some of the suggestions you may receive MIGHT affect your voice. This is a fine line. Only you can judge this. Lastly, working with a good critique partner / beta reader will be positive experience. They will give you feedback on what you do well. They will point out what you need to improve and give suggestions on how to improve it. They shouldn't just re-write whole sections. When the story/book is complete, remember to thank them for their efforts. Just like authors, they like to be respected too. (I also always make a point of thanking those who've assisted in my books.)

If unsure, invest in some good quality editing books.

### Time to Bake The Cake

**WARNING!** Before you put your book up on any fanfic site, be aware that many publishers consider this your first rights and that technically your book is now published.

Still with me? Excellent! So you've had your work critiqued and beta'ed. Brilliant. This is NOT the end of the line, though. Not by a long shot. You now have 2 questions to ask. Will I go with a traditional publisher or will I look at self-publishing? Two very different mediums for publishing.

### Let's look at Traditional Publishing first.

A traditional publisher will expect you to do several very important things before they will sign your work.

- Learn exactly what genres they publish and read their guidelines. - Not every house accepts every type of book.

- If they say they don't accept YA... then DO NOT send them your YA manuscript on the "off chance" that they might pick it up.

- If they say no, it's usually for a reason. All you will do is make them cross. This is NOT a good look and it WILL NOT help you get published. Remember, just like any other professional — THEY TALK TO EACH OTHER!

- Read specifically what they want in your submission. Do they want a Publicity Plan? 3 Chapters? A full synopsis in 3 pages or less? If you don't understand, find someone who is with them and ask. Follow their guidelines. They are there so they can streamline the reading process.

- Find out if they accept only paper-based submissions or only e-submissions. I know this sound lame... but it happens and editors DO NOT like their rules being ignored.

- Oh and if you don't like their guidelines, don't whinge about it online. Yes, I have seen this happen. Nothing—I repeat, Nothing—puts off like a publisher seeing that on a website.

- Make sure your work is as polished as it can be. Trust me. You will thank me for this one down the track!

- A traditional publisher WILL NOT require you to pay for editing/ cover art or anything else. The rule of thumb is...

IMPORTANT — If you pay, it's vanity press!

*There's More With Imogene Nix*

# *Self-Publishing Is Different*

### Self-Publishing is different. Way different.

There is still a fair degree of stigma attached to self-publishing, no matter that there are many well prepared and successful self-published books. To date, I only have a few self-published titles. Why? Because I'm not really interested in doing it all myself.

That's exactly what self-publishing is about. Doing it on your own, your own way.

If you self-publish... PLEASE do yourself a favour and shell out for decent cover art and decent editing.

### Developmental editing can help you fix things like these:

- Holes in your plot
- Story threads that dead-end
- Main characters that fail to captivate
- Secondary characters that should be scrapped or given a larger role
- Decisions about voice (first-person vs. third, close vs. omniscient, etc.)
- Order of the scenes
- Flow of action and pacing
- And many others

## Line editing focuses on the sentence or paragraph level, rather than the broad story-scope of your novel.

It's about refining sentence structure and flow to make your writing both more readable and more pleasurable to read.

Line editing can help you fix things like these:

- Wordiness

- Awkward sentence structures

- Other issues that make your writing feel "unpolished." Line editing is what helps you go from the first sentence to the second one below:

    –Hands trembling, she stared at her sister's number at the top of the call list on the screen, and after hesitating another moment, sent the call through.

    –Hands trembling, she stared at her sister's number for a moment, then sent the call through.

## Copy editing is about grammar, punctuation, and proper word usage.

It's the kind of editing you'd pull out your Chicago Manual of Style to do. Here are the types of questions you might ask yourself when doing a copy edit:

- Should I use "which" or "that"?

- Did I use punctuation correctly in the dialogue?

- Should that be a comma or a semicolon?

- And a zillion others

Note that in the publishing world, the terms line editing and copy editing are sometimes used interchangeably, as they are closely related and often done by the same person or as a single step in the editing process. Some line editing may also be done during a developmental edit. So if you hire an editor, be sure you're clear on what services he or she is offering.

## Proofreading is the final step in the editing process and results in the final don't-touch-it-again draft.

This is where you catch spelling mistakes, typos, missing words, isolated punctuation errors, and the like. It's the step that requires the most attention to detail, so if you're doing it on your own work, it's often essential to set the manuscript aside for a period of time so you can approach it with fresh eyes. Another helpful trick is to read your work aloud at a slow, measured pace.

For many writers, line editing, copy editing, and proofreading fall under a single umbrella called "being anal." : ) If this is your stance, you might want to consider hiring a professional. Agents, publishers, and the reading public want a flawless product. So if you'd rather leave the nit-picking to those who enjoy it, no problem! But in the long run, you'll be glad you didn't cut any corners.

## How to find a "good" editor?

Ask people you know who have been successfully self-published. This does not mean ask Mary-Jo down the road who vanity published a book that her gran, her sister and the dog bought. It means find people with a good reputation and steady or growing sales. Ask respected self-published authors who they used to edit their book. There are places you can go to gain recommendations:

Contact the Australian Society of Editors or even find them on the internet. Ask around other published authors - go with those who have a record of decent sales. They'll be able to nominate decent editors.

**<u>Editing isn't cheap, but it is a case of You Get What You Pay For.</u>**

Be prepared to fork out. A tiny fact: My recent under 8K title cost $120 to edit. Like I said, not cheap, but worth it, to ensure the title isn't a mess that you will always regret and that will come back to haunt you.

Examples of bad or no editing.

- 1. "Yes, I do want a cookie with my milk. I would also like a sandwich."

  "Chocolate chip okay?

  "Yes, chocolate chip would be good. Please give me two chocolate chip cookies and one very large glass of milk. I will eat them at the kitchen table. I cannot sit at the dining room table."

  "You talk kinda funny for a kid."

  "I am only four. What do you think a four-year-old child should sound like? Maybe you are the one who talks kind of funny."

I can hear you now. What's wrong with this? First up, I don't have a clue of who said what. There are no hints. Just dialogue. I also don't know where they are. I don't feel any connection to the characters. It's just dialogue.

- 2. "Yeah, Jack ran after Melanie," Arthur told us. "Jack tried to get her to turn around. Jack ran down the street, calling Melanie's name, determined she'd listen to Jack's pleas one time." Arthur snapped his fingers. Nodded. Yeah, Jack would get her to listen. Jack had that way about him. Melanie didn't stand a chance. Not with Jack dogging her that way.

When you are editing, you need to be clear who is the person watching and keep it in that. Here, the scene has multiple points of view. We also have run on paragraphs. I find myself asking, is it Arthur who snapped his fingers? Who else is in the scene?

Many questions, mostly unanswered. To be honest, these people either didn't use an editor, or whoever did edit them didn't have a clue.

**Rule of thumb**: If you want to be taken seriously in this industry, don't skimp. Pay for an editor. Your career will thank you. Take a look at these- The Editor's Blog, 'Don't Publish That Book', and 'What People Talk About'.

Earlier on, you saw a sample of editing that was done for me. Here is a before and after of a grab from one of my stories:

### Example of work before editing...

The beat of the music filled the air. Her eardrums felt like they were undulating in time with the rhythmic beating of drums pounding out of the black stereo unit in the corner of the lounge room. The floor boards bucked beneath her bare feet as Karina slowly put the glass on the side table. The table top was littered with the remains of chips, beer bottles and half full glasses.

The house was a shambles after sixty of her closest friends had finally departed from her farewell party. Not that she was really going anywhere too exciting. It was, after all, only an interstate transfer, not to the moon. But her friends had been adamant and who was she to turn down an opportunity to party?

### Example of work after editing...

The beat of the music filled the air. Her eardrums felt like they were undulating in time with the rhythmic beating of drums pounding out of the black stereo unit in the corner of the lounge room. The floor boards bucked beneath her bare feet as Karina cautiously put the glass on the side table next to the remains of chips, beer bottles and half-full glasses.

The house was a shambles after sixty of her closest friends had finally departed from her farewell party. Not that she was going anywhere too exciting. It was, after all, only an interstate transfer, not to the moon. But her friends were adamant they should celebrate her transfer and who was she to turn down an opportunity to party?

If you've published traditionally, thankfully most of this is dealt with, but there are other pitfalls, such as editors who will "change" your voice. And yes, this does happen.

This is a really broad subject and there isn't enough room here to deal with that. However, needless to say, the best way to cope with this is to work with reputable publishing companies. Have a strong advocate (Queensland Writers Centre, Romance Writers of Australia, etc., on whom you can call, and an experienced published mentor.)

It's not uncommon to find that you go through a number of edits (or drafts of edits) for that matter. I regularly have 4 or more runs with my editors. Why? Because as you pick up one set of issues and correct them, it often raises another batch. Sometimes the wording just isn't right and needs a couple of tweaks. It could be that questions are raised that need to be answered and you just aren't able to explain it correctly in the first pass. There is NO right or wrong number of passes.

## **TIP!**

Learn to use the REVIEW or TRACK CHANGES function on your computer. Your editor will likely use it, as will your critique partners and Beta readers. YouTube have a number of tutorials on that, or grab a copy of the latest Microsoft Word How To manual.

*Self-Publishing is Different With Imogene Nix*

# *Cover Art*

Now it's time to consider covers. They are the first and in many cases best opportunity for selling your title to the masses. There is lots of information on the web about effective cover art and the result of poor cover art choices.

Cover Art is the first thing a reader will look at, when considering your book. There have been a number of articles written about this over the last few years. Cautionary tales are told to every beginning author. In essence, though, it pays to remember that if you have a scrappy second rate cover, then that will reflect badly on your book.

Let's take a moment to consider how to choose the cover you think would be best for your title. Say you wrote a book about spanners. Let's call this fictional title "The History and Evolution of Spanners." You've spent years researching, writing and editing this tome. It's ground breaking! Then you put a photo of a flower on the cover. Your readers take one look and rear back in horror. Yes, this is an over the top situation, but I came up with that particular scenario to highlight the incongruity of the choice. Cover Art should be indicative of the contents of the title. A dark tale usually sees dark tones of reds, blacks and greys. A light contemporary might have pastel tones on the cover.

There's so much more to cover art than the colours though. Firstly, where did you get your image from? Did you trawl the internet? Have you considered the copyright issues with the graphics. If you purchased it from a stock image site, did you ensure you used the correct license?

In the last few years, there has been a crackdown on unauthorised use of images with bloggers, authors and artists being called to account for the use of images they have no legal right to.

Next up, you need to work out what size cover you have and whether your image has sufficient definition to be reproduced. There's nothing worse than a grainy cover because you've used a cheap small image, rather than paying for the correct size.

Will you be producing a print cover as well as digitally producing your title? You see, if you are planning on using it for both, the situation with the licensing of your images have just increased in terms of problems. See, most licenses allow for a certain amount of use... impressions or printing. Whether it is used for online or printed matter. All authors should learn about this, so that they can protect themselves from difficulties that may arise in this area.

Lastly, do you have adequate design skills to ensure that the book looks suitably engaging. An awesome article was produced by Courtney Milan. Instead of reinventing the wheel, I suggest you take five minutes and peruse the blog entry. Dear Author Cover Designs

If you want to see some examples of bad cover art, feel free to visit my blog as Imogene Nix.

For the record... A Sapphire For Karina in its final format cost me a grand total of $120 to publish via Smashwords and CreateSpace. I make a fairly decent percentage of the cover price. This was for full service and a friend who is a cover artist actually having the image on hand ready to use.

I could have got away with a Pre-made book cover for as little as $35. You just need to do some looking around, using a reputable person who specialises in my genre.

Lists of cover artists: Flickr Photos Pandora or Listings Book Covers Market A quick Google search will bring up a heap of others.

### So what comes next with Imogene?

We are getting to the end of the publishing journey. You've got a decent cover, shelled out for good editing and are ready to go to the next step. It's time to launch that baby out into the world. If it's traditionally published, your publishing house will arrange that step for you, which is fabulous. If not, and you're self-publishing, watch out! There are a couple more pitfalls ahead!

## TIP! DO NOT fall into the traps of a vanity publisher.

These are the ones you have to pay $$ for service. There are tons out there, they'll take your money and you might get 50 - 100 books but they will be super expensive for what you get. They won't publicise you. They won't do anything except print it, and they won't be rigorous in anything they do on your behalf.

According to The Australia Society of Authors: 'Vanity publishers tend not to call themselves vanity publishers. Instead, they describe their services as "joint venture publishing" or "partnership publishing'.

### Questions to ask

Always make sure you are getting true value for any costs you are asked to meet, by asking the right questions.

- Who subscribes to the publication? If they can't tell you this, then I'd be more than concerned that it's purely an "out there, don't care" enterprise. They should, at the least, be able to give an idea of how many opens to electronic emails and who their target audience is.

- What are the distribution arrangements? No, I don't just mean who they send emails to. I am talking about which shops can you find your books in? How do they advertise your book?

- What is the date of the publication? Who else will be releasing on the same day? If there is a load on the same day, be wary that they aren't just pushing books out there like an author mill.

- Is there any money back guarantee? Be very wary with this. Many will tell you how easy it is to get a refund, but when you actually need to do it, it's nigh on impossible. Yes, I know of people this happened to.

- What exactly are you getting for your money? You need to think long and hard about the benefit of the service they are using.

- How many will be printed? Limited print run? POD is not as badly thought of as it used to be, but check the price point to ensure it's competitive. Don't forget to consider the shipping costs too, and exchange rates if you are working with an overseas company.

### **What to watch for.**

Unethical vanity publishers share some common characteristics.

- Their products are expensive and of little real value.

- They will often insist that you must act immediately if you want to take advantage of their 'tremendous' deal.

- When the product is not published on schedule, consumers will be given a string of excuses for the delay.

- They will not get a review in any reputable publication.

- They will not get your story or poem into mainstream distribution.

Be very wary before handing over any payment. It might be worth considering any of the below mentioned services. They'll tell you upfront what you get for your money. As with anything, I would suggest that you read and research this side of the business so you know EXACTLY what you are signing up for.

Before you "invest" in anything though, do some basic investigation work. This includes taking a look at the following resources: Preditors and Editors and Absolute Write Forums

At the end of the day, it's up to you to do your research, find a suitable platform. Just don't jump because it sounds too good to be true. Take your time. Do your checks.

## **TIP!**

Booksellers (bookshops etc.) DO NOT like to buy in paperback and hard cover versions of self-published and POD (Print On Demand) titles.

### **The reason for this is two-fold.**

- 1. When a bookstore (particularly the larger ones) orders books in they are on a "return and refund" basis with the distributors. Most bookstores will only carry books for a limited period of time, before they become "dead." They can't afford to have books filling spaces. So they "return them" to the wholesaler as unsold titles.
- 2. POD is print on demand. Once purchased they have them in stock till they sell. They can't send them back for a refund. They tend to only order these in as required.

You may be able to get them to take them On Spec...

### **The marketing of your book MUST have a multi-pronged approach.**

You will need a social media platform. My advice is to pick 2 or 3 and work them. Just be careful not to overwork them and become a spammer. I know authors who did that and were quickly deleted from people's lists.

- Find groups that will promote your work to readers.
- Get a blog together and share "hops" - that is where you "visit" each other's blogs with interviews etc.,
- Consider targeted advertising... just remember you need to recoup every $$ spent.
- You can visit markets and sell your book direct to the public.
- Try conventions that deal with the genre you are writing in.

- Perhaps radio or television are in your sights?

Just ensure that whatever cost you have to pay is covered by the sales, after the cost of production of your book, is covered.

### Advertising with Imogene

As we get to the point of launching your title, you need to create a marketing plan. Again, if you are with a traditional publisher, you may find they will give you advice, make opportunities available to you... If not, you will likely need to do this yourself.

Among the basics you will need to create:

    I. Twitter Account

    II. A Facebook "Like" page.

    III. If you're a nom de plume, I would also suggest a profile page in that name.

    IV. A website — preferably with a blog.

Remember each of these is considered a professional platform. If you intend to go down this path, particularly if this is your first title and you intend to publish more, then you need to invest time and resources into building a following.

Whatever you put up there, be aware that this is your business. What you display on the page is an indicator of how professional you consider your publishing. I would strongly recommend you do not use it for personal recollections, political comments etc., You want to be taken seriously? Act like you would at work.

A lot of authors use teaser cards, which they place on their Facebook "like" pages. Again, think of the one image that saves 1000 words addage.

If you plan to create paperbacks, sometimes it could be worthwhile creating books marks. They can be quite expensive, however, there are cheap ways to get value for your money. It is worthwhile seeing if you can get things like this into your local libraries. Ensure you have your website address clearly marked, (and updated, showing where your title can be purchased!)

Goodreads. While I really don't enjoy the site, it is worthwhile listing your titles on there. Reviews are as important to an author as sales.

### TIP! Be braced.

Once your book is out there, someone somewhere will review it. Some of them get a little personal. I had one recently that said my writing was bad and that as I had so many books, likely I didn't want to get better. Ouch!! We all get bad reviews. It's part of the business you wade into when you start this process. Immaterial of how bad they are, there is one cardinal rule we all try to subscribe to. DO NOT ENGAGE NEGATIVE REVIEWERS!

Sadly, there are trolls out there. The whole reason for their existence, that I've managed to understand, is to drag authors down and beat them with negativity. Above all, authors are professionals. No matter what we think of the persons review, there is nothing to be gained from by engaging in a "you don't get my book" argument. In fact, authors who usually engage in this behaviour, find to their detriment, that it makes things worse. Much worse.

Some suggested reading includes: Writers Win Avoid Trolls and Self Pub Authors When Trolls Attack.

Lastly, I suggest setting up a newsletter, joining a writing group (either face to face or online... or even better, both!). I use Mailchimp, as it's free for me at this point. When you tip over a certain number of subscribers, then costs apply. It's certainly worth taking a look at that.

### TIP! Who owns your Social Media when you pass away?

As silly as it sounds, it is up to you, the author of your social media enterprise, to ensure that this resource (and that's exactly what it is) is protected into the future. When next updating your will, remember to include the following rights. Be clear as to who will be entitled to royalties, the assignment of rights and ownership of your social media and written resources.

## Where to from now with Imogene

Your book is out, you've partied like there's no tomorrow at the launch and it's time to take care of the loose ends. These are things every author should know about and consider.

## IRS and ATO.

If you choose to publish internationally you need to do some serious thinking. If your book is published in the U.S.A. you need either an ITIN (Individual Taxpayer Identification Number) or an EIN (Employer Identification Number) from the IRS (Internal Revenue Service.

Now there have been some changes lately, which allows places like Amazon to accept your ABN, but I still recommend going down the track of gaining an ITIN if you intend to publish more than one title. You can only get an ITIN with assistance from your publisher. If you choose the Self Published route through Amazon or Smashwords, you need to do some research before you apply.

Check out the following pages for information: Smashwords Support, Amazon Self-Publishing, USA Tax Department

Check this is THE most up-to-date version before using it!!! I would also suggest, as I'm not an accountant or in any position to give specific and targeted advice, that you consult a professional with regards to what is claimable, whether you should consider an ABN and/or register for GST.

## ISBN.

The International Standard Book Number is a 13-digit number that uniquely identifies books and book-like products published internationally. While an ISBN is not mandatory, and does not provide copyright on a work, it is the principal world-wide ordering device for the international book trade and library market. If you publish with Smashwords, you do have an opportunity to use their ISBN. Amazon you must pay for your own.

*Cover Art With Imogene Nix*

# *Imogene's Final Words*

Cool! You've come to the end of Imogene's information, but this is just a sample of the information you need to be aware of. In today's world, being an author is no longer just about writing the book.

It's about researching what you need to do, creating a following and being ready to act quickly, depending on what changes occur in the publishing world. You must market, protect and if necessary, copyright (USA) your title.

The revolution is not over. Should you wish to look further into the world of publishing, there is a world of information out there, and many wonderful authors willing to work with you. All you need to do is ask.

Most of us are happy to talk to new authors, if you just ask the questions. Good luck on your journey! I wish you every success!

If you wish to know more about my forms of advertising, feel free to take a look at my Website - imogenenix.net

## TITLES TO HELP YOU SUCCEED!

Imogene's Book Suggestions:
- The Elements of Style - William Strunk, Jr. ISBN 9780486447988
- Self-Editing for Fiction Writers - Renni Browne & Dave King.
- ISBN 9780060545697
- Eats Shoots & Leaves - Lynne Truss. ISBN 9781592402038

# *What's Next?*

So, you've written your book, given it the best possible editing, and still can't decide if self-publishing is the best way for you to go next?

**Let's take one more look at the options.**

- Send your book to an agent who will represent you?
- Submit directly to one, or more, publishers?
- Self-publish from the start?

**When Is Self-Publishing the Best Option?**

- Book doesn't fit editor and agent requirements
- Book has a specific niche market
- Author has connections in that niche market
- Book's audience is too small for traditional publishers
- You don't like the terms of publishing contracts
- You don't like handing over control
- You don't like handing over a chunk of your income
- You want daily access to your sales figures
- You want higher royalty rates
- You want to sell immediately

- You don't want to wait for an elusive contract
- You want to relaunch an old book
- You want to design your own cover
- You know what market suits your book
- You are happy to do your own marketing

**Look at this list and ask yourself who you'd prefer to do these tasks.**

You, or a publisher?
- Editing and proofreading
- Cover art
- Writing teaser or back cover copy (back cover blurb)
- Writing your author bio
- Final layout and production of the physical book or digital book files
- Adding excerpts from your other books into the back
- Purchasing an ISBN
- Setting prices
- Arranging promotion
- Requesting quotes from big-name authors – optional
- Sending out copies for review – optional

You might think it looks easier to hand everything over to a publisher, but the book market is far too competitive these day for your publisher have time to do all these tasks.

YOU will fill in a form for directives for cover art.

YOU will write your author biography

YOU will write your back cover blurb, which your editor may, or may not, review and make suggestions.

Edits will be sent back to you once, twice, maybe three times for you to work on. You might need to get all your own review quotes, if you want them.

And then there is book promotion. Many present day authors are shocked to discover that the publisher does very little in the way of promotion. Selling your book to the public is more or less your problem.

This is why so many authors self-publish now. If you're doing the lion's share of the hard work, why not keep most of your earnings in your own pocket?

<u>**Mark off your personal writing goals.**</u>

<u>**Is it ...**</u>

- Publishing your family history?
- Publishing your children's book?
- Writing and selling more than one children's book?
- Publishing your mother's recipes?
- inning writing awards?
- Seeing your book in a bookstore?

- Knowing your book is for sale at online retailers
- Having 20 books published under your name?
- Top of a retailer genre bestseller list e.g. Amazon
- World bestseller lists e.g. The New York Times
- Earning tens of thousands of dollars a year?
- Speaking at conferences about your writing journey?

**<u>Reaching your personal goals as an author already makes you a success.</u>**

And remember that goals can change from year to year. So enjoy your success and celebrate every goal you achieve, small or big. Then, if you want more, put your head down and keep working. Becoming a successful author is about talent, drive, hard work, and sometimes tears.

Perhaps you'd like to be a hybrid author? Hybrid authors have a combination of self-published books plus some traditionally published books. Perhaps you'd like and income while you aim for a contract with an agent or publishing house, or both. It's very easy to self-publish one, or more, books while you continue submitting other work to editors and agents, as traditional publishing is a much slower journey. Perhaps you'd like to self-publish from the start and then reset your goals late.

Though self-publishing is not a get-rich-quick scheme. Nor is it a place to sell substandard books, because readers are very discerning.

**<u>Checklist Before You Begin Self-Publishing</u>**

By writing down your answers, you'll have an ongoing checklist. Or, if you only plan on publishing one book, you'll have a short list of tasks to tick off.

- What do you already know about self-publishing?
- What do you need to learn more about?
- How many books do you plan to publish?
- Have you made a yearly writing plan?
- Have you ever run your own business before?
- Do you have a business plan?
- Do you have money for a cover artist and editor?
- Will book sales become your primary income?
- Do you have a niche market?
- Do you already have a readership?
- Will you write under your legal name, pseudonym, or publishing company?
- Are you able to secure the privacy of your real name?
- Would you like print, digital, audio and/or foreign translations?

### **Where does the author end and the publisher begin?**

In self-publishing, you're going to experience a constant tug between your author responsibilities and your publisher responsibilities. In case you're unclear on what each of these are, let me share my perspective:

- Author: writes the best book ever and participates in promoting the book.
- Publisher: manages production, distribution and promotion to make money for both publisher and author.

But don't feel too daunted. Doing these things for yourself gives you an enormous self-confidence boost and you are able to control how much, or how little, you prefer to do.

### Pen Names - Yes or No?

Most authors prefer to use a pen name, or several names, to publish their books. In this day and age, it pays to do everything you can to protect your privacy.

Reasons for using a pen name vary, but generally if you write books that you don't want your work colleagues or family to know about because they are erotic, use a pen name, or even two. Perhaps you co-author books and need another pseudonym, or you want readers to recognize and connect your name with a specific genre and rating e.g. Young Adult.

Self-publishing used to have a bad name and was often thought of as another type of Vanity Press, so authors used alternate names to disguise the fact that they were the publisher. Thankfully those days have gone, especially now that authors such as Belle Andre and Marie Force have spoken up about their yearly earnings and how they make a lot of money because they put out a quality product.

And yes, you can register and/or copyright your book under your pen name. No need to have your real name displayed anywhere, unless you really want to. There have been several cases in recent years of either authors being stalked by fans or of crazy authors stalking book bloggers. So stay safe and use a pen name and never put your home address on the web.

Before deciding on your pen name, do a few simple searches to see how many other individuals or businesses are using the same name. Do a Google search, search on Amazon, and if you want to ensure that no one else is using that name, think about buying it as a domain name. Try Go Daddy for this.

You can legally call yourself, and your writing company, any name, but if you want to fully protect yourself you might consider setting up a company name, although this can be expensive. Some authors outside of the U.S.A still use an American Limited Liability Company (LLC) to protect their identity and to pay taxes and move money, and this is good if you are doing Boxed Sets of books with authors form different countries, but it isn't cheap.

For Australians, other options are to become a Sole Trader and apply for an Australian Business Number (ABN), or register yourself as an Australian company.

### Places you must be as an author.

These things are essential for every author, whether self-published or not, but are even more important if you are trying to build an author brand and readership by yourself.

**Amazon Author Profile** – This is very important as it is one of the main places that a reader will find you, so you should be sure to go to each different country and make sure your information has been added to your name in each place. Countries are listed at the very bottom of the page under your book at amazon, and you can log in and make an account in each place. Amazon says you should add your biography of roughly 100 words, profile photo, connect your blog, Twitter etc., upload photos and videos, on the Author Page tab in Author Central. And check that all your books appear and if any are missing, add them in the Books tab.

**Goodreads** – The Goodreads Author Program is free and is designed to help authors reach their readers. This is the perfect place for new and established authors to promote their books. So make sure your profile is up to date, with your biography, photo, web site, your books and books that you are reading. Add the Goodreads Author widget to your personal website or blog to show off reviews of your books, or use a Print Book as a book giveaway and join groups or discussions about books in the genre your write. To Sign up as an author on Goodreads - Sign in and search for yourself and click on your published author name. The author name is listed below the title of your book in the search results. Clicking on your name takes you to your basic author profile page which has your name at the top and "author profile" to the right of your name and is part of their database of books and authors. Scroll down to the bottom of the page. Click "Is this you?" to send a request to join the Author Program.

Google Alerts – Set up Google alerts for both your name and the names of your books. That way, Google will alert you if your book has been added to a web site somewhere, and to be really sure you catch them all, do a regular Google check yourself. Enter your name and books into Google Search and see what pops up. You'll be surprised how often Google picks up things around the web about you that you weren't aware of.

## Book Keeping

- Track income, expenses and cash flow
- Excel spreadsheets for each book are the easiest
- Months are columns of spreadsheet.
- Rows show distributors, numbers sold, and earnings per sale

**Create a list of expenses to launch and maintain your publishing business.**

- Establishing a DBA or fictitious name (optional)
- • Forming a LLC (optional)
- Applying for an EIN or ITIN with the IRS (may be necessary for non-U.S. residents to sell through U.S. companies like Amazon and Apple) = free
- Website domain and web hosting (recommended)

- Newsletter software e.g. Mail chimp
- Various social media profiles
- Equipment purchases (do you need a new computer?)
- Software purchases (do you need to upgrade Word or buy a formatting software?)
- Writer organization memberships
- Attendance at conferences and book signings
- Subscriptions/dues incurred with promotion sites, writing organizations, magazines, etc.

**Add to this list the expenses that are specific to self-publishing your book(s)**

Break these expenses down by book by book

- Registering copyright
- ISBN(s)
- Editing
- Cover Art
- Formatting
- • Distribution Fees
- Book or Series website (optional)
- Ads online or in print media (optional)

## What sorts of things are tax deductions for a self-published author?

- Fees paid to freelancers
- Fonts or images you buy for your book production
- Fees associated with distribution (for example, some distributors offer ISBN or premium distribution options with a fee)
- Copyright fees
- ISBNs
- Business cards, bookmarks, swag
- Ads you place online or in publications
- Giveaways of physical copies of your book
- Giveaways of gift cards
- Research or craft books you buy
- Research trips you might make
- • Online classes or workshops
- Conferences, book signings
- Memberships in writing organizations
- Office supplies
- Travel to meetings and conferences
- Contest entries
- Postage
- Website expenses for your author website

## More Book Cover Tips

A good cover is essential to grab a reader's attention because there is huge competition with so many thousands of new books released each month. So here are few more tips for your book cover.

Advice from the experts, and from iBook's, is to Keep it Simple! E.g. Author Name, Book Title, and a high resolution image. No clutter, and don't make it so obscure that readers can't guess the genre of your story. Keep your covers consistent because 'Branding' is a great tool for authors to get their name and their books remembered.

Retailers have, finally, made it easier and you can now create one larger sized eBook cover that will suit most major retailers. Size must be more than 1400 pixels on the shorter side for Smashwords, so if you create one of 1600 x 2400 pixels in JPEG it should work for all. Though All Romance needs 'exactly' 200 by 300.

For a Print cover, you need a front cover, back cover, and spine, and the spine isn't easy to do without a pretty close estimate of your page numbers.

If you're looking for a book cover designer, you might like to look at my list on Diigo, though please excuse the mess. Go to Diigo.com/SuziLove and search for Book Covers.

Or if you're looking for faster and cheaper version, there are many sites that do Pre Made Covers and put an exact price on them. They add your name and your book title and you are ready to go. Go to Diigo.com/Suzi Love and search for Pre-made.

**When looking for a book cover, make sure it meets these requirements.**

- Conveys genre and tone of your book

- Clear to a shopper, even in thumbnail view
- Visible even in black and white

### Trying Your Own Book Covers?

If you have experience with digital images, you might like to try you own book cover, or at least make some of your own marketing material.

**Photoshop**. This is the most expansive software, though it is probably the most expensive. Though there is a monthly payment option via Adobe.

**Gimp**. A free photo editing software. Gimp is complicated to learn but a good alternative to Photoshop. Brian Jackson has blog posts on installing and using GIMP. There are Gimp Tutorials on You Tube and all over the web. Book Cover Pro software is an option to purchase.

**Shopping for Images**. Many websites offer 'free' images, usually defined as "free for non-commercial use." Make sure you read the terms for every image and understand where and how often you can use them. You can buy 'stock' images for between $5.00 and $75.00  Some might need an Extended License to extends the royalty free option over a certain number.

**More about Royalty Free here**: iStock Photos

Creative Commons is a way of copyrighting that allows for certain uses of images

### Suggestions for Finding Cover Images:

- iStockphoto
- Dreamstime
- 123RF

- BigStock
- Stock.XCHNG
- Morgue File
- Public Domain Pictures
- Shutterstock
- Fotolia
- Library of Congress public domain images

And take a look at my Diigo list for Photos and images.

## Book Release Dates

- No right or wrong time
- Try to time for holidays and seasons.
- Early-mid November – fewer books bought as holiday plans take over
- Summer is a season when digital books may slump, or soar.
- Kids are out of school and parents might have less free time.
- Or, more books might be bought for beach reading
- Remember that retailers close during the end of year holidays.
- If you are releasing for a specific holiday, upload at least 30 days before.

- Books about Christmas? Launch before the end of November, or earlier.
- Books that tie into Mother's Day? Release a month before.
- Many traditional publishers schedule new releases to go on sale on Tuesdays.
- If your aim is to hit the USA Today or New York Times bestseller lists, try releasing your book on a Sunday or Monday to sneak in a full week of sales.

## Groups All about Writing and Publishing

The Alliance of Independent Authors (ALLi) is an amazing non-profit professional association for self-published authors who self-publish. They do video interviews with experts and posts on self-publishing topics. All sorts of valuable advice available.

All the largest countries have their own romance writers associations e.g. Romance Writers Australia and Romance Writers America. Google them to find one in your country. Many towns have local writing groups.

If you write crime books, there is a worldwide crime and mystery association which has conferences and advice. Australian Crime Writers and Crime Writers UK

For history lovers, try the Australian Historical Association or one of the numerous local associations in America and Great Britain

The Non-Fiction Association has wonderful information on how to publish your non-fiction book, plus resources, contests, and webinars for authors.

*What's Next? With Suzi Love*

# Self-Publishing Nitty-Gritty

**Time to get into the where, when, and for how much you will sell your book.**

### Setting Up Your Business

If you're an Australian author, read up about ABN's and see if the terms apply to you. And ABN is easy to apply for but if you only intend publishing one book many of these legal aspects won't apply to you.

Maybe you'd like to look into one of these options to help protect your books and publishing efforts, though you don't have to do any of it. Most authors are Sole Proprietors.

- DBA (Sole Proprietorship)
- LLC (Limited Liability Company)
- Corporation

A limited liability Company (LLC) is a separate legal entity you create for your business, and even if you are not in the US, many self-publishers chose to create a company to help protect your privacy and your personal assets. LLC is much simpler to form and maintain than a Corporation because one person can be a LLC.

### What About Tax? Shudder!

A large portion of all book's sales are made in the USA. Therefore, you might need to apply for one of these via the U.S. Internal Revenue

Service or IRS.

- Employer Identification Number (EIN)
- Individual Taxpayer Indentifcation Number (ITIN)

If you live outside the U.S.A., retailers, such as Amazon, can pay you your royalties and withhold a small amount of tax, depending on your country's tax treaty with the USA. But as these rules change often, please check your own country's rules for these.

The American IRS website allows you to apply for an EIN online. It's free, and this is another way to prove your "ownership" of your DBA/ FN.

## **ISBNs**

These are numbers that register your books, and you need a separate one for eBook, print book, and audio. Prices vary widely in different countries, but in Australia they are much cheaper than in the US and bought from Bowker either singly or in bulk, and in NZ they are free.

No retailers require them to self-publish. Amazon gives your book an Amazon number anyway, and CreateSpace will give you one for your print book for free. But, having an ISBN may up your Google ranking and help other vendors pull out search data for your book. Also, if your book does well, an ISBN can help you get on the best-seller lists for NYTimes, USA Today, and other lists.

Personally, I like to be able quote the ISBN in the front of my books if reporting a copyright violation to a pirate site, and knowing that Bowker keeps a register of all ISBNs and who purchased them.

Take a look at Bowker or My Identifiers and Australian ISBN Information

### **Scheduling your book release.**

Make a plan for your book and try to stick to it, as many of the best editors and cover artists are booked up months in advance.

**Book your editor.** This is essential. Readers are very fussy these days about the quality of books.

**Book your Cover.** Start early and know what you have in mind. Send examples of how you want it to look, and include a list of things like hair colour for your heroine and hero, setting if you want a background image eg City, country, beach. Work out your 'Branding' eg using consistent font for your author name.

**Book Formatter.** If you don't want to tackle formatting yourself, send your book to one of the many places that do formatting for you.

**Print Copy Review.** Allow time to format for print and then to review your book before ordering print copies.

### Write Blurb and Back cover copy.

**Gather metadata.** Keep all your book information in one place to make it easier to upload to book bloggers, retailers, discounted book sites, promotion sites. You'll need your title, ISBN, Amazon ASIN, Author Bio, direct links to retailers, perhaps a retailer ID number for your account, cover image, author photo etc.

**Upload to retailers.** This can vary enormously in time. Amazon is very fast and may have your book available within a day if there are no problems. They also send you're an email if they discover spelling errors. Smashwords are usually fast to show books on their own site, but before they send to other retailers in the Premium Catalogue e.g. Barnes and Noble, Kobo, Apple etc., your book will go into 'Review', as some of the extra sites are extremely fussy about covers and formats.

**Organize Marketing.** Work out what suits you best.

**Pre Orders at all sites, or only some?** Amazon only counts pre-orders once, but iBooks counts Pre-orders when they are ordered and paid for and when they are released, so double whammy.

### A Face Book Release Party?

**Discounted opening price at retailers?** If so, book some of the book deal sites for promo on certain days at your introductory price.

Take a look at my Diigo lists for Suzi Love's Free and Deal sites. Diigo.com/SuziLove

### Your Publishing Schedule

- Revise the book with developmental or content editing.
- Get started on your cover production.
- Arrange copyediting and/or proofreading.
- Think about print and/or digital formatting.
- Write your back cover copy and gather metadata.
- Register copyright and/or ISBNs
- Work out your launch date
- Decide on dates to upload to retailers or aggregator
- Decide whether to have Pre-Orders or not
- Get started with your marketing ideas.

### A Word About Pre-Orders

Most of the retailers now allow Pre-Orders of your book, but information changes frequently so read each retailer's help information and then decide about doing Pre-Orders.

You can upload your basic metadata up to 364 days in advance of your release date, depending on specific retailer requirements, and then add your cover art and ePub file later. Start with a simple book description of at least 50 words, and then expand it.

Upload a book sample so readers can read a teaser of your upcoming release. Describe your whole series, include social media links, your full book list, behind-the-scenes copy, etc. Once you release your book, you can replace this custom sample if you wish.

Smashwords or Draft2Digital, as aggregators, have information on their sites re Pre-Orders their interfaces may be built to handle pre-order information and distribution.

If you're writing a series, Apple (iBooks) do great series marketing. So, if you've written Book 1 and expect to release Books 2 and 3 in the next year, get them uploaded for pre-orders.

# *Getting Your Book Ready*

### **Accepted Formats**

Retailers have extensive guidelines and ways to preview your formatted book

- Microsoft Word (or any text file) is commonly accepted, though you may need to 'unformat' bits

- EPUB is a standard e-book file format

- Paid formatting services generally offer EPUB and MOBI files

- PDF is one of the most difficult file formats to convert

- Word documents uploaded to Smashwords go through their 'meatgrinder' conversion

- This creates a variety of free e-book files for you

- DRM (digital rights management) is supposed to prevent piracy, or illegal copying and distribution of your e-book after is sold

- DRM is not reader friendly and should not be used

- Industry standard e-book format, EPUB, does not use DRM

- Amazon Kindle uses a proprietary format with DRM and will automatically lock your book

- But you can make your e-book available in other formats through other services

- iBooks Author tool creates e-books in a proprietary format that only an iPad or iPhone can view

## N.B.

Your books will always be pirated, no matter if you tick the box to add DRM to your files at retailers. DRM stops readers sharing their legitimately bought books between their devices and is therefore a nuisance for most readers, though it doesn't stop pirates who can strip DRM from a book in seconds. My advice it therefore to not apply DRM as it's better to allow readers to share the book between their computers and mobile devices and even with friends. You may lose one sale but pick up more consistent readers.

One common strategy among authors is to use Amazon's Kindle Direct Publishing (KDP) combined with Smashwords (which distributes to all major e-book retailers except Kindle). You can probably reach 95%+ of your market with that approach, if not 100%.

## Book Creation Tools To Look At

**Scrivener** - can compile your book and export it in an ePub format. If you've set things up correctly, the ePub will be valid and acceptable at all retailers, including Apple (who is the most finicky).

**Vellum** - Wonderful software to compose your chapters and files into an awesome ebook format.

**Jutoh** - software you can purchase to help with formatting.

**Dragon Speak** – For dictating your book instead of typing.

## Creating Your Front Pages

**N.B.** Not All Need To Be included)

- Table of Contents (TOC), navigable if an eBook
- Title page - book title and author name
- Copyright statement:- Copyright © YEAR by AUTHOR NAME
- Copyright statement for Cover and Cover Art, if necessary
- Copyright statement for back of book excerpt
- Editors, formatters, interior book designers acknowledged
- Trademarks acknowledged.
- ISBN for each version of Print, eBook, Audio
- Rights statement, disclaimer that the book is a work of fiction
- Book blurb or back cover copy
- Dedication

### Copyright Declaration Example:-

"This book is a work of fiction. Names, characters, places, brands, media, and incidents are either products of the author's imagination or used fictitiously. Any resemblance to actual events, locales, or persons, living or dead, is entirely coincidental. All rights reserved. No part of this book may be reproduced, stored in a retrieval system, or transmitted in any form or by any means, electronic, mechanical, or otherwise, without expressed written permission from the author. The author acknowledges the trademark status and trademark owners of various products referenced in this work of fiction, which have been used without permission. The publication/use of these trademarks is not authorised, associated with, or sponsored by the trademark owners."

## Creating Your Back Pages

**N.B.** Not All Need To Be included
- Acknowledgement of anyone who helped the author
- Notes for Readers
- Other books list
- Author biography
- Links to social media
- Second notice to sign up for your website newsletter
- Excerpt from your other books
- Excerpt of books by your writing friends
- Glossary, map, pictures
- Readers guide for book clubs

### Blurb, or Back Cover Copy, or Book Description

Your blurb and/or back cover copy needs to be catchy and use as many metadata hooks as possible because most readers are attracted to a book by covers and the blurb. But catchy blurbs are very difficult to write. Try these tips to make the blurb you put with your book at retailers easy to understand, and leave a reader wanting their questions answered.

Five things to remember – make it short, no sub-plots, add tension, mention only two characters, and promise an exciting read. USE THE SCOPE ACRONYM:- Setting, Conflict, Objective, Possible Solution, Emotional Promise.

- At the end, add your website link minus the http://.

- Add a line like this: 'To learn more about .... and her books and to be the first to hear about contests and giveaways, join her newsletter found on her website.'

- Do not attempt to make your website address an active link. Most retailers don't allow clickable links in the book description.

- Editorial Reviews or quotes go before or after your blurb. But be certain you have permission from whoever wrote the review to quote it.

- Only include professional reviews, not simply a customer review.

- Try to include some metadata: categories, keywords and tags.

## What Do You Know About Metadata?

Metadata is used to help categorize your book and the key to good metadata is consistency. Retailers, libraries, distributors, bookstores, and buyers rely on metadata to tell them about your book. The two most important metadata elements are categories and keywords.

## The metadata to include inside your book is:

- Title

- Author

- Publisher

- Copyright

- Publication Date

- ISBN
- Language
- Series Name and Number
- Book Description and Keywords.

### Where do you key in metadata?

Some metadata is embedded within the eBook when an ePub or Mobi file is created, such as title, author, ISBN, publication date, copyright info, publisher and primary book category. Before you press publish, check that everything is included.

### What do you know about keywords?

Descriptions and keywords show your book's content and help readers search for your book on retailers and in libraries. Along with factors like sales history and Best Sellers Rank, keywords can boost your placement in search results on retailers, and more exposure means more books sold. To plan your keywords, think like a book reader doing a search and read each retailers allowances.

- Use up to seven keywords or short phrases
- Combine keywords in the most logical search order
- Separate phrases with commas
- Read suggestions at retailer sites
- Experiment
- Switch them around often

## What do you know about categories?

Categories fit within the defined list of BISAC, Subject Headings or Subject Codes List. It's a standard used to categorize books based on topical content. The Subject Heading applied to a book can determine where the work is shelved in a brick and mortar store or the genre(s) under which it can be searched for in an internal database.

Book Industry Study Group has all the Subject Headings for choosing your categories.

On this list, there is a Fiction category and a Juvenile Fiction category. Within Juvenile Fiction, there are plenty of kid's categories, but there are also some Young Adult categories, such as Dystopian.

- Retailers all support BISAC in a limited way
- But no two retailers are exactly the same.
- Choose up to 5 categories.
- Not all retail sites will allow that many, but a few do.
- Keywords should match search terms that readers use when looking to read a book like yours.
- Think about hooks or tropes that make your book popular.

**N.B.** Amazon has a help section explaining categories and keywords, because getting these right makes a huge difference to your book's discoverability. Search at Amazon for Categories Help and another article, Make Your Book More Discoverable with Keywords.

## Release Dates For Your Book

Remember, there is no right or wrong time and best book launch dates vary widely from country to country, so do what suits you and your book.

### Here are a few tips to help you decide.

- Try to time for holidays and seasons.
- November – fewer books bought as holiday plans take over
- Summer is a season when digital books may slump, or soar.
- Kids are out of school and parents might have less free time.
- Or, more books might be bought for beach reading
- Remember that retailers close during the end of year holidays.
- If you are releasing for a specific holiday, upload at least 30 days before.
- Books about Christmas? Launch before the end of November, or earlier.
- Books that tie into Mother's Day? Release a month before.
- Many traditional publishers schedule new releases to go on sale on Tuesdays.
- If your aim is to hit the USA Today or New York Times bestseller lists, try releasing your book on a Sunday or Monday to sneak in a full week of sales.

### Making changes to your e-book after it goes on sale

If you're working directly with retailers (e.g., Amazon and Barnes & Noble), you can upload new and revised files as often as you like—they don't care. Same goes with Smashwords. However, if you're using a multiple-channel distributor other than Smashwords, you will likely have to pay fees to make changes

### More Book Cover Tips

A good cover is essential to grab a reader's attention because there is huge competition with so many thousands of new books released each month. So here are few more tips for your book cover. Advice from the experts, and from iBooks, is to Keep it Simple! Eg Author Name, Book Title, and a high resolution image. No clutter, and don't make it so obscure that readers can't guess the genre of your story. Keep your covers consistent because 'Branding' is a great tool for authors to get their name and their books remembered.

Retailers have, finally, made it easier and you can now create one larger sized eBook cover that will suit the majority of them. Size must be more than 1400 pixels on the shorter side for Smashwords, so if you create one of 1600 x 2400 pixels in JPEG it should work for all. Though All Romance needs 'exactly' 200 by 300.

For a Print cover, you need a front cover, back cover, and spine, though the spine isn't easy to do until you have a pretty close estimate of the number of pages in your book.

If you're looking for a book cover designer, you might like to look at my list on Diigo, though please excuse the mess. Go to Diigo.com/SuziLove and search for Book Covers.

Or if you're looking for faster and cheaper version, there are many sites that do Pre Made Covers and put an exact price on them. They add your name and your book title and you are ready to go. Go to Diigo.com/Suzi Love and search for Pre-made.

**When looking for a book cover, make sure it meets these requirements.**

- Conveys genre and tone of your book
- Clear to a shopper, even in thumbnail view
- Visible even in black and white.

### Trying Your Own Book Covers?

If you have some experience with digital images, you might like to try you own book cover, or at least make some of your own marketing material.

**Photoshop**. This is the most expansive software, though it is probably the most expensive. Though there is a monthly payment option via Adobe.

**Gimp**. A free photo editing software. Gimp is complicated to learn but a good alternative to Photoshop. Brian Jackson has blog posts on installing and using GIMP. An there are Gimp Tutorials on You Tube and all over the web. Book Cover Pro software is an option to purchase. Info here:

http://www.bookcoverpro.com/order/

**Shopping for Images**. Many websites offer 'free' images, usually defined as "free for non-commercial use." Make sure you read the terms for every image and understand where and how often you can use them. You can buy 'stock' images for between $5.00 and $75.00. Some might need an Extended License to extends the royalty free option over a certain number.

**More about Royalty Free here**:

iStockPhoto istockphoto.com

Creative Commons is a way of copyrighting that allows for certain uses of images. **creativecommons.org**

### Suggestions for Finding Cover Images:

- iStockphoto
- Dreamstime
- 123RF,BigStock
- Stock.XCHNG
- Morgue File
- Public Domain Pictures
- Shutterstock
- Fotolia
- Library of Congress public domain images

# Selling Your Book

No retailers will ever reveal their actual market share of eBooks and since a lot of authors have stopped using ISBN numbers, the numbers below are only estimates from those who follow this closely.

**Amazon** - still the biggest earning retailer for most authors and we can upload directly to Amazon, which means that you can earn 70% royalties if your book is between $2.99 and $9.99, and 35% for shorter and cheaper books.

Amazon Kindle Direct Publishing (KDP) has over 60% of market and 25% of revenues on Amazon come from self-published titles in the USA. There is also KDP Select, which locks your book into Amazon exclusively for three months, but the benefit is that the book might get extra exposure. Your book also then goes into Kindle Unlimited where 'Borrows' earn money, and this could be a good option for short stories or shorter books. Files can be uploaded as word documents and are then converted to Mobi files, the type used for Kindles.

**Google Play** – Growing rapidly and will continue to grow because mobile phones numbers in countries like India are exploding, and therefore eBooks will also be in demand. It's not easy to upload here, but if you gather all your bank, tax, and book information and tackle it, one day it will pay off for you.

**iBooks** – Apple iBook Store also holds roughly 25% of the eBook market (estimation) and Australians weren't previously able to upload directly, but this has changed if you hold an ABN can meet their requirements. You must have a Mac to upload, an iTunes Connect account, and need to download iTunes Producer. You can then upload an EPub File (under 2 GB) and earn royalties directly. Until now, Australians have always used Smashwords or Draft 2 Digital to upload, which means losing a small amount of royalties.

**Barnes and Noble** – Known as Nook Press, has perhaps 25% of eBook markets. If you are outside the USA, you cannot upload directly to Nook but you can use a distributor.

**Kobo** – Kobo Writing Life has single digits market share and authors outside of the USA can now upload directly, or use a distributor.

**Smashwords** – For authors living outside the U.S., Smashwords is an aggregator for Barnes and Noble, Kobo, Apple, Overdrive, etc., but you pay a small percentage of royalties.

**All Romance (aRe/OmniLit)** – For romance books.

**BookBaby** – Allows you to decide what kind of financial arrangement you prefer, based on the level of service you need. You can (a) pay $0 upfront, get eBook formatting/conversion, and give them a percentage of your sales (similar to Smashwords), or (b) you can pay a flat fee up front and keep 100% of your net sales if you're able to provide ready-to-go ebook files.

**And then there is Diesel**… and dozens more.

## Main Things To Ask About Retailers

Are they Exclusive, or Non-Exclusive? Generally, book retailers are non-exclusive, meaning you can sell your book at other places at the same time.

Are there exceptions? Yes, two of them. Amazon's Kindle Select needs 3 months exclusivity and their terms are 90 days, but your book is included in Kindle Unlimited, a book subscription plan. Apple's iBooks Author Tool creates special edition books using a Mac. However, exclusivity applies only to these editions and not editions of your book created elsewhere.

Do you control the prices? In general, yes. Though Amazon's policy is to not sell books below 99 cents and they will price match if they find your book sold elsewhere for less. The plus side of this policy is that you can force Amazon to make your book free if it is reported to be free at other retailers.

Are they free to use? Amazon's Kindle Direct Publishing, Barnes and Noble's Nook Press, Apple's iBook store, Kobo, Google Play are all free to use. Then they take a cut of your sales and give you 60-70%. Smashwords pays you 85% on sales directly through Smashwords and approximately 60% on sales through retailers.

## Print On Demand

Print on demand (POD) is a great idea for self-published authors and there are several options, although CreateSpace is probably the most popular.

### CreateSpace

Easy to Use

Offers expanded distribution to libraries via Baker and Taylor

Linked to Amazon so has better royalty rate

No upfront costs to upload your book.

Sets wholesale discounts at 20% for the CreateSpace store, 40% for Amazon, and 60% for expanded distribution.

### Lightning Source (Ingram Content Group)

- Distribution through Ingram, Baker & Taylor
- Distribution to international distributors and retailers
- Distribution to other retailers
- Yearly Charge

## IngramSpark

- Digital and POD distribution to retail and library partners worldwide.
- Setup fee for print books plus yearly distribution fee.
- If you order 50 copies of print book within 60 days of publication, IngramSpark credits back your $49 setup fee.
- Often offer discount codes on set up and print fees
- Wholesale discount choices for POD distribution, 55% and 40%

## Lulu

- Hard cover and paperback printing
- Global REACH distribution via the Ingram catalog.
- Review their global REACH terms first.

**Library Distribution.** Thousands of libraries world-wide continue to add books to their collections in print, large-print, audio and digital formats. But reaching them is often difficult and knowing if it's worthwhile or not financially is still up for debate. And if you choose to create a large-print (or foreign translation) edition, are you willing to donate a copy to select libraries? Many libraries subscribe to the major distributors, such as Ingram or Baker & Taylor.

**Distribution Into Libraries**. Smashwords has library distribution as one of its Premium Catalogue options. Like CreateSpace, you need to use the Smashwords ISBN to take advantage of library distribution. Visit Smashwords and read more about their Premium Catalogue and their extended distribution because this soften changes. OverDrive distributes digital content such as eBooks and audio books to libraries, schools and retailers.

## Audio Books

- Audible.com - Owned by Amazon
- Distributes to iTunes, Amazon and other online retailers.
- Audible doesn't publish indie audio books, but they have an arm that works with self-published authors
- ACX Audiobook Creation Exchange

### Two options for producing an audio book.

- You find a narrator to partner with you. Narrator shares royalties of your audio book sales.
- Or, you hire a narrator and pay them a mutually agreed-upon fee. Narrator has no claim on your royalties.

Sites that charge fees for various services.

For authors living outside the U.S., you might need an aggregator to gain wider distribution to retailers such as Barnes and Noble, Kobo, Apple, Overdrive, and many more. The most commonly used aggregators are Smashwords and Draft 2 Digital. They take a small percentage of your royalties but are an easy way to get your book available at all retailers.

Draft2Digital: https://www.draft2digital.com

Smashwords (http://www.smashwords.com)

### Benefits of Using an Aggregator, such as Smashwords, if you live out of the USA.

1. After Premium distribution approval, your eBook will be available on Barnes & Noble, Kobo, Apple, Page Foundry, Baker & Taylor, Blio, txtr, Library Direct, Baker-Taylor, Axis360, OverDrive, Flipkart, Oyster and Scribd.

2. Link on your publisher's dashboard for every with a list of SEO entries for each title

3. Download copies of your own book in any one 8 different file formats at any time.

4. Coupons for doing eBook promotions by giving out a discount code

5. Dashboard has 'Affiliate Settings' which may earn some extra money

### Book Pricing for Digital Books

- Kobo, Apple and Google Play will allow you to set your selling price to $0.00

- Barnes and Noble won't allow you to set prices unless you distribute to them via Smashwords to them.

- Amazon continues to price match.

- Books priced lower than $2.99 earn a 35-45% royalty from most retailers.

- Apple continues to pay 70% royalty for books priced as low as 99¢.

- Apple pricing in the U.S. always ends in .99. This may make it hard to set the exact same price across all the retailers.

- Major retailers allow prices to be set in U.S. dollars and then automatically converted to other currencies

- But you can also override these preset conversions and customize pricing by country or currency.

- Depending on whether you upload to retailers directly or use an aggregator, it can take from hours to days for prices change on various retailers
- Most self-published books sell for $2.99 to $7.99
- Shorter books are priced lower
- Full-length books are often $4.99 to $5.99 range
- Discounting may help sell more books, which moves you up in ranking on retailer sites. This visibility can increase your sales again
- Once you have several books in a series, try offering the first book for free.

This article from Digital Book World analyzes the latest thinking about pricing ebooks.

'Digital Book World Value of an eBook'

### Tracking Your Sales.

Thankfully, most retailers now have reports and graphs to let you see exactly how many books you sell each day, plus there are sites that track your daily book rankings e.g. Novel Rank. Or send you a daily email update on which books you sold and where. eg Book Trackr.

- With Amazon's KDP, B&N's Nook Press, Kobo, and Google Play you can track your sales in real time.
- Log in to your various accounts and see if you've sold books.
- But don't do this constantly, or you'll go crazy.
- Apple updates sales daily.
- For ranking, Amazon updates continuously

- Barnes and Noble's ranking is updated daily unless your book is in the top 1,000, then it's hourly.

- Kobo's ranking updates at least twice per day

- Apple doesn't use a ranking feature.

- Google Play has downloadable reports, so definitely only once per day there.

### **Getting Paid**

The major eBook distributors distribute earned royalties on a monthly basis, though the payments are on a lag time of 45-60 days. So, sales for January can be seen usually on daily 'Reports' in our retailer dashboard and you receive payment at the middle or end of March (45-60 days following the end of January).

Some pay by direct deposit and some via PayPal. When you set up your payment information, you can usually request payment in your preferred currency. In that case, payment can be set up via Paypal or an American bank and Payoneer is excellent for this. Payoneer runs via the Bank of America, can link to your bank account and your Paypal account, so you can move money in various currencies and only earn small transaction fees.

Be aware that Amazon allows eBook returns, supposedly within 7 days, and there will always be some readers who take advantage of that and return your book, either read or unread, so you will see that on your Dashboard too.

### **Tips to help you sell your book.**

Book marketing is hard work, competitive, and can be very expensive. Learning how to market a book economically and effectively is a learning curve.

Whether traditionally published or self-publishing, every author needs to be able to sell their own book without making readers hate you.

- Write the best book possible.
- Set up a Google Alert for your name and book name so you get notified every time you are mentioned on the web.
- Start 'branding' yourself: logo, theme, slogan, etc.
- Set up a website, even if it's very basic. WordPress is easy.
- Start blogging on your website
- Update news about your release dates, retailers, formats, etc.
- Set up an account and claim your writing name on lots of social media sites.
- Even if you don't use them all, do Twitter, Facebook, Goodreads, Pinterest, Google+, Tumblr, Instagram, etc.
- Social media is a necessity, like it or not, so get stuck into it.
- But don't aggravate readers with constant 'buy my book' messages
- Pick 2-3-4 places you enjoy and engage with people
- Find your niche market and talk to people
- Be positive and upbeat and never get involved in arguments.
- Set a time limit each day for marketing
- Pay for some exposure but budget and set limits.
- Write another book.
- And another.

## Book Not Selling?

- Change your book's description or blurb
- Change your book's keywords
- Change your categories
- Change your price.

## Great information on improving book sales and other self-publishing topics here:

- The Creative Penn
- Russell Blake
- Jane Friedman
- Passive Guy
- Digital Book Today
- GalleyCat
- Author E.M.S.

## Reviews of your book.

- Many reviewers post book reviews on Amazon, B&N, Goodreads and Smashwords, iBooks, Kobo, Nook, Google Play.
- There are sites to upload digital copies of your books where can download your book for free. e.g. InstaFreebie

- Don't stress about reviews

***Selling Your Book With Suzi Love***

# *Copyright*

### Copyright, DMCA, and Plagiarism

Copyright is a legal concept, enacted by most governments, giving the creator of an original work exclusive rights to it, usually for a limited time.

One type of copyright infringement occurs when someone copies all or part of a copyrighted work without permission. Copyright material may include literary works, images, videos, music, etc.

If you feel that your rights as a copyright owner have been violated, you can try to contact the offender first and see if you can settle the copyright infringement between yourselves. If the party you have to deal with is not overly co-operative or doesn't have contact info readily available, there are other steps that you can take to deal with a copyright issue. If an agreement can't be reached between the two parties involved, then you may have to take your case to court and have them settle it.

Although your original work is protected by copyright laws, guarding your copyrighted material is your responsibility.

### From Imogene Nix

**COPYRIGHT & DMCA**. The Digital Millenium Copyright Act is an American act, instituted to stop the act of pirating of books. For authors/musicians/movie makers this is one of the biggest drains financially that we all face. A book may take me in the region of 3000 hours to write. (That's 6 months working 5 days a week for 10 hours a day)

'In all seriousness, if I earned $15 an hour (which is less than at IGA) I would earn $45 000 yet I know very few authors who make that much. Most authors earn between 7% & 30% of the cover price per book. That means on a $5.99 book, I get $1.79 per copy sold. I need to sell 25 140 to cover a living wage.

Each time a book is pirated... that's $1.79 less.

So how do we cope with that? Most authors set Google alerts to keep track of their titles and send DMCA take down notification to sites each time our books are uploaded. It's time consuming, because there is certain information we must give in each notification. I would suggest that everyone takes a few minutes to look up the DMCA information.

If your books are published in Australia, you are automatically covered by our copyright rules. In the US, I pay each and every time to ensure I get coverage under the act.'

## More About Copyright From

### Suzi Love

Copywriting is a tricky subject, like tax, because laws may be different from country to country. But remember, your book is under copyright protection the moment you write it down. Proving you own copyright may be a much longer process.

Copyrighting your book is not going to deter pirates from stealing it, or from buying one copy legitimately and then distributing to many countries where pirates thrive. And being with a large publishing company makes no difference either, as probably more of those books are pirated because of author name recognition and more people wanting those expensive books.

The World Intellectual Property Organization (WIPO) represents 180+ countries that all recognize copyright without the formality of registration. There is no single "international copyright," but if you live in one of these countries, your rights are protected in all the member countries.

Copyright gives the owner of copyright the exclusive right to do and to authorize others to do the following:-

- reproduce the work in copies or phonorecord

- prepare derivative works based upon the work

- distribute copies or phonorecords of the work to the public by sale or other transfer of ownership, or by rental, lease, or lending

- perform the work publicly, in the case of literary, musical, dramatic, and choreographic works, pantomimes, and motion pictures and other audio visual works

- display the work publicly, in the case of literary, musical, dramatic, and choreographic works, pantomimes, and pictorial, graphic, or sculptural works, including the individual images of a motion picture or other audiovisual work

- perform the work publicly (in the case of sound recordings) by means of a digital audio transmission

## More Thoughts On Book Copyright

- The general consensus seems to be to register copyright first in the country where the book is published.

- By registering copyright in your home country, you may be able to battle any infringement from your home country, but you may not be eligible for as much "coverage."

- By registering U.S. copyright, in the event that you file a lawsuit, it will be filed in U.S. courts and you'll be eligible to collect damages according to U.S. laws.

- Since copyrights last beyond your death, consider how to handle your copyrights as part of your estate.

- If your book includes works in the public domain, references to famous works, or you don't know if material is still under copyright, you should research your copyright status.

- Foe copyright advice, take a look at Columbia University, USA.

### Sample DMCA:

### Subject: Notice of Copyright Infringement

The copyrighted work at issue is the text that appears on my website under my books …

The URLs where our copyrighted material is located include website … and website …

You can reach me at my email … for further information or clarification. My phone number is … and my mailing address is … The email address of the website owner, who has reprinted our content illegally, is …

I have a good faith belief that use of the copyrighted materials described above as allegedly infringing is not authorized by the copyright owner, its agent, or the law.

I swear, under penalty of perjury, that the information in the notification is accurate and that I am the copyright owner or am authorized to act on behalf of the owner of an exclusive right that is allegedly infringed.

Mary Smith Author,

May, 2016

**Plagiarism** is the "wrongful appropriation" and "stealing and publication" of another author's "language, thoughts, ideas, or expressions" and the representation of them as one's own original work.

We sincerely hope that this never happens to you, but if you suspect plagiarism of your book, try this tool to test it. Grammarly Plagiarism

Checker.

*Copyright With Imogene Nix and Suzi Love*

# *Formatting*

### PDF for Print Books

Portable Document Format (PDF) is the standard format for creating print books and documents. Creating a print book requires that you format it to standard print book sizes and provide a PDF file to the printer. Every program from Word to InDesign, PowerPoint to Photoshop, can export in PDF format and be printed exactly as is to paper or digital.

### Standard EPUB

The EPUB formatting option is the standard choice. Everyone in digital publishing uses the EPUB standard, except for Amazon. EPUB can be read on Apple devices, Barnes and Noble Nook, and via apps like Adobe Digital Editions. EPUB gives you access to the biggest e-book stores on the market.

### Amazon Kindle (MOBI)

Amazon created a formatting option separate from (but based on) EPUB — Amazon Kindle's MOBI. Readers can download the Amazon Kindle app onto any e-reading device, and MOBI-formatted e-books will be accessible.

### Formatting Advice by Sassie Lewis

It's easier to dress something that's already naked.

So you've been through the daunting processes of plotting—or pantsing if you're like me. Beta readers, editors (we all know our former English teacher is not a qualified editor, right?) cover artists and proofreaders. And now it's almost time to upload your precious.

Wait! You want it to fit in and not be picked on by all the big bad books on Amazon, don't you? Knew you'd say yes. So lets ensure your baby doesn't get hit with meta-data, coding or formatting errors. And dammit, because by now you're broke and you can't afford my awesome services, so you're going to have to work this out yourself. Never fear, I am foremost an author and just because you can't afford me doesn't mean I'm not going to help you out.

### Basic formatting

Emphasis on the basic. Anything more complicated and we'd need a bigger book. The formatting tips here will allow you to upload to any and all ePublishers.

### Things you will need.

1. Microsoft Word:

If you don't have it, get it. If you can't get it, borrow it. And if you can't do either of those two, well you're shit-outta luck and should contact Sassie's Formatting ;)

Unfortunately if you are not using a professional formatting program, Microsoft Word—not the free version—is a must and all the following steps will be in reference to using it.

2. Calibre:

This is a free program and you are going to want to download this. https://calibre-ebook.com

3. Alcohol:

Trust me, if this is your first foray into formatting you are going to want it. Remember to drink and format responsibly.

4. Love thy Save button:

After EVERY step go hit that save button.

## Now we're ready to actually start formatting

**Step 1**: Duplicate and save a new version of your file. Why? Because, trust me, shit happens.

**Step 2**: Make sure there are no edits or comments remaining throughout the document and turn OFF track change/edits

**Step 3**: In the top ribbon select the nonprint character button. Once you do that, at the end of each paragraph you will see this (¶) symbol. This feature will show you all formatting. Returns, double spacing, tabs etc. with their own identifying symbol.

**Step 4**: Top ribbon, select Review. In there, open the 'review pane'. Here you should see a symbol that looks like a magnifying glass. Select this option.

**Step 5**: This is how you find and replace all that nasty formatting. Things like double spacing between words, smart quotations, etc. Go ahead and replace everything which needs replacing. I strongly suggest doing step 5 before adding 'styles'. If you have any problems there are hundreds of YouTube videos which walk you through 'find and replace'.

**Step 6**: Add page breaks between chapters.

Place the cursor in front of the first word of your chapter. In ribbon under 'insert' find insert page break. NOT section break.

**Step 7**: Remove extra 'returns'. The only time there should be a blank space between paragraphs is when there's a mini scene break. (Or if you're writing nonfiction; it's also the only time these parentheses are allowed.)

**Step 8**: Adding styles. 'Style' is found under 'format'. Rather than working off a style that is already in Word, create your own by selecting 'new'. I always find it best to name the 'style' for what it is e.g. Chapter heading, first, body, scene break and any other specialized formatting you'd like to add. I also use all uppercase when naming them, and I'll explain why later.

<u>Note:</u> Most platforms are very particular on font and size; so as a rule stick with Times New Roman 12point, with either 1.15 or 1.5 line spacing with 'justified' position.

- **Step 8a**: Name your style — leave Style Type as 'paragraph', and leave 'style based on' as Normal. * Pick your font. As I've said, it's best to stick with Times New Roman 12 point

- **Step 8b**: Check all the options at the bottom. Add to template, Add to Quick Style list, Automatically update.

**Step 9**: At the very bottom of this box is a button called 'Format'. It has a drop-down option, where you select 'Paragraph'. This will open a new box. Here is where you fine-tune your style/s. Things like first line indent, paragraph spacing, text alignment, etc. Have a little play but the standard is:

- First line indent – 1.25cm (0.49 inches)

- Justified text

- No paragraph spacing before or after — exceptions are when you're formatting 'Headers' or other specialized styles i.e., Text messages, letters. Here I always put 24 points before and after. (12 points = 1-line space)

**Step 10**: Press 'OK' at the bottom of the screen, which brings you back to your first screen. Press OK again.

**Step 11**: Press 'APPLY'. You have now created a style.

## Applying your Style/s

Along the lower ribbon you should see a section which says 'Styles'. To the side of that is what looks to be a piece of paper with this symbol ¶ on it. Go ahead and hit that button.

This panel has all the styles you've created, plus those already designed by Word. (This is why I name the styles I've designed in UPPERCASE. They now stand out amongst the dozens which Word recommends.) It also gives you the option to 'Show Styles Guides', a great feature which places a color panel at the side of your page showing the style applied to each paragraph. And there is also 'Show Direct Formatting', a useful tool that puts things like italics in a blue colored bubble.

But back to telling you how to apply those styles you've made to the manuscript.

**Step 1**: Place your cursor into any paragraph you wish to format.

**Step 2**: In that 'Style' box floating somewhere at the side of your screen, find the style you want to apply and then click it.

**Step 3**: Do step 1 and 2 over and over and over again until you've formatted every paragraph within your manuscript.

*YIPPEE* you're almost finished. Now put the booze down and let's do the chapter headers. I'm going to make this one easy for you.

### Chapter Headings.

Forget all the fancy fonts, Amazon will not hold them. The Zon will change it to one of their acceptable typefaces and if you don't know what you're doing you also run the risk of screwing up all your hard work and having your book knocked back from other platforms. So for those who are new to this, I strongly suggest using one of the premade styles in Word. e.g. 'Subtitle'.

## The end is almost near

We're almost done, I promise. That program I told you at the beginning you'd need, Calibre? Well now is the time to use it.

I'm not going to walk you step-by-step through this but just give you the quick overview.

    1: Add your file to Calibre.

    2: Export as an ePub.

Simple as. What you've just done is added all that metadata you need and made yourself a pretty eBook. THIS ePub is the file you're going to upload to Amazon etc.

As I've mentioned there are hundreds of videos around to help you through this daunting process, but if you're ever stuck give me a holler at sassie.lewis@gmail.com for professional formatting.

*Thanks to Sassie Lewis for this information.*

## Previewing Your Formatted Files

It is important to preview your ePub and Mobi files before publishing, whether you made them or had a formatter make them. To read the files, use one of these free softwares on your computer (or use your eReader device): Adobe Digital Editions to read ePubs, and Kindle Previewer software to read the Mobi format.

You can also use free software to review your downloaded files, change them into different formats, and check metadata.

- Sigil for ePubs

- Calibre for Mobis and ePubs (Free)

- Jutoh (not free, but can edit ePubs and Mobis)

## CreateSpace Formatting

If you are using images in your book, incorporate images into your PDF. This is best done by embedding an image in Word, and then converting it. Be aware that CreateSpace wants images that are high resolution (300 dpi or greater).

## *Suzi's Final Words*

Finally, have fun with your self-publishing.

It can be very exciting to release your book knowing that you have had total control and that the book of your heart is going out to readers in the best possible condition.

Don't be despondent if your first sales are less than you'd expected, because until you have more than one book for sale readers won't be able to pick up your backlist books. And backlist sales make your earnings grow.

After you have a few books for sale, you'll see more consistent sales and you'll begin to earn good royalties.

If you refer back often to our Cheat Sheets and Checklists, you'll stay on track and love becoming a self-published author.

I certainly do!

# *Cheat Sheets and Your Notes*

### Cheat Sheet For Agents.

- Agents approach a range of editors on your behalf
- Find you the best deal for your book
- Ensure your contract offers best possible outcome
- Take 15% of your royalties
- Hard to get accepted by good agents
- May take a long time

### Cheat Sheet For Publishers

- Submissions go into the 'slush pile'
- An editor requested submission gets fast tracked
- Agent submissions get fast tracked
- Some still pay advances, small or large, but not many
- Publisher takes largest share of money
- Advances are earned back before royalties begin
- May, or may not, put your book into print

- May take a long time until release date

## Cheat Sheet For Publisher Contracts

- Advances, especially large ones, are rare in today's publishing world
- Commonly now a publisher offers no advance but a slightly higher royalty rate than previous traditional publishers offered
- Beware Vanity Press - small publisher who asks you for money to cover part, or all, publishing costs. RUN AWAY!
- Signing a contract sounds exciting but signing away all rights can be a disaster.
- Check the publisher first: Financially sound? Large stable of authors? Sell a lot of books? Good rankings for their books on Amazon? On Goodreads?
- Publishers are going out of business, or merging, every week.
- Never give away your book rights without knowing exactly what you get in return.
- Be careful giving away rights to print, translations, audio etc.
- Do your homework. Go to Writer Beware.

## Before you sign with a publisher or agent.

- Do a Google search
- Read everything you can about them.
- Check their credentials

- Take a look at these places
- Writer Beware
- Writer Unboxed
- Agent and Editor Wishlist
- The Book Designer

### Cheat Sheet For ISBNs

- ISBN = International Standard Book Number
- Universally accepted number defines a book as a product in the marketplace
- Identifies book title and edition for inventorying, buying, and retailing purposes
- Not always required for digital books, but definitely recommended
- Information goes into a central database for retailers, libraries, and media outlets
- Information can consistently be recorded with each retailer.
- Consistently recorded metadata improves your book's visibility

- Without one, your book may not be eligible for global distribution via retailers

- Without one, sales reporting to outside sources (Best Seller Lists) may be limited

- Print, digital, and audio versions need individual ISBNs

- Can be bought in lots of ten or a single

- Some countries don't charge e.g. New Zealand.

- Some countries are well priced e.g. Australia

- Some countries charge more e.g. USA

### Where do you get ISBNs?

- Bowker sites (called My Identifiers)

- Australia -National Library works with Thorpe-Bowker. Buy ISBNs at my identifiers.com.au Get Information at The Australian isbn agency. nla.gov.au

- USA - My Identifiers.com

- U.K - Nielsenbook.co.uk manages ISBNs

- New Zealand- National Library manages ISBNs Plus deposit of your book natlib.govt.nz Publishers and authors. (In NZ, ISBNs are free)

### Bar Codes

- Not usually necessary to purchase one

- Print-on-demand retailers e.g. CreateSpace, automatically print a bar code on your cover.

## Cheat Sheet For Blurb, or Back Cover Copy

- This must to be catchy
- Use as many metadata hooks as possible
- Add your website link minus the http://.
- Add a line like this: To learn more about …. and her books and to be the first to hear about contests and giveaways, join her newsletter found on her website."
- Do not attempt to make your website address an active link. Most retailers don't allow clickable links in the book description.
- Editorial Reviews or quotes before or after your blurb. Be sure you have permission from whoever wrote the review to quote it on your sales page.
- Only include professional reviews, not simply a customer review.
- Your author bio.
- Metadata: book price, categories, keywords, tags.

## Cheat Sheet For Places to Sell Your Book

- Kindle Direct Publishing (KDP) by Amazon
- Writing Life by Kobo
- iBooks /iTunes by Apple
- GooglePlay

- NOOK Press by Barnes and Noble
- Smashwords
- BookBaby

## Cheat Sheet For Getting Paid Royalties

- Major eBook distributors generate earning reports monthly
- Lag time of 45-60 days covers accounting and book returns.
- Amazon still allows eBook returns within 7 days
- Most retailers pay by direct deposit, PayPal, Payoneer etc.
- A few may still mail out royalties
- Posted royalties mean long delays and currency conversion
- Each retailer pays specific royalties
- Generally 70% if priced between 2.99 and 12.99
- Generally between 35%-40% if under $2.99 or over $12.99

## Tips For Choosing Your Writing Name

Reasons to publish under a different name
- to protect your and your family's privacy
- You and another author co-write books under a pseudonym.
- Branding your books under a publisher name

- Not appearing to be self-published

## Tips on Piracy

If you are concerned about your book showing up in Google Alerts on pirate site frequently, try one of these paid websites that track book pirates. DMCA and Muso.

## Cheat Sheet For DMCA

## Simplified Copyright Infringement Letter.

Use this as a base and add any relevant information

To whom it may concern:

I am writing to inform you that the book,………, is being distributed in violation of my copyrights. I,………, have copyrighted the work.

I have not authorized the distribution of my work on this site.

(put URL/URLs for site here)

I swear, under penalty of perjury, that the information in the notification is accurate and that I am the copyright owner or am authorized to act on behalf of the owner of an exclusive right that is allegedly infringed.

Sincerely,

Author Name

Email address

Web Address

Phone Numbers

# *Checklists For Self-Publishing*

## **Checklist Before You Begin Self-Publishing**

By writing down your answers, you'll have an ongoing checklist. Or, if you only plan on publishing one book, you'll have a short checklist to do and tick off.

- What do you already know about self-publishing?
- What do you need to learn more about?
- How many books do you plan to publish?
- Have you made a yearly writing plan?
- Have you ever run your own business before?
- Do you have a business plan?
- Do you have money for a cover artist and editor?
- Will book sales become your primary income?
- Do you have a niche market?
- Do you already have a readership?
- Will you write under your legal name, pseudonym, or publishing company?
- Are you able to secure the privacy of your real name?
- Would you like print, digital, audio and/or foreign translations?

## **Your Publishing Schedule**

- Revise the book
- developmental or content editing.
- Get started on your cover production.
- Arrange copyediting and/or proofreading.
- Think about print and/or digital formatting.
- Write your back cover copy and gather metadata.
- Register copyright and/or ISBNs
- Work out your launch date
- Decide on dates to upload to retailers or aggregator
- Decide whether to have Pre-Orders or not
- Get started with your marketing ideas.

## **Cover Checklist**

- Conveys genre and tone of your book
- Clear to a quick shopper
- Clear in thumbnail view on phones etc.
- Visible even in black and white.
- Author name must be largest
- Book title second largest
- Request all files from cover designer

- Check who owns the cover, you or cover creator
- Print cover needs front cover, back cover, spine
- eBook cover at least 1600 x 2400 pixels in JPEG
- All Romance eBook cover 'exactly' 200 by 300 pixels

### Checklist For Marketing

- Start promotion 2-4 weeks before book launch date
- Notify free promotion sites.
- Pay for some promotion if needed
- Notify Face book groups of your launch date
- Advertise cover reveal on your twitter feed.
- Advertise book launch date on your twitter feed.
- Notify your local community
- Schedule a Goodreads Giveaway
- Decide whether you want to guest post on blogs
- Research guest post and guest interview guidelines.
- Approach some book bloggers.
- Send some targeted Goodreads ads
- Arrange a launch day book signing or celebration

# *About Imogene Nix*

Imogene Nix is a multi-published author of both erotic romance and town histories. Imogene is published in a range of romance genres including Paranormal, Science Fiction and Contemporary. She is mainly published in the UK and USA due to the nature of her tales.

In 2000, Imogene dipped her toe into the publishing world with Thargomindah - The Town By The Bulloo, written and self-published in conjunction with the Thargomindah Historical Society and RADF. This successful venture was the first step in a publishing history that spans many years and quite a few books.

In 2011, Imogene Nix was born at the Australian Romance Readers Conference. Returning from the conference enthused, Imogene sat down and worked tirelessly for 3 months culminating in the books Starline. This book became the first in a trilogy titled, "Warriors of the Elector." In fact, she has completed six entire series.

Imogene has successfully been contracted for twenty-five titles and self-published three others, under this pseudonym. She has also completed another three and is, like many of her contemporaries, seeking homes for these books—with at least one likely to be self-published once ready. Sex, Love & Aliens Vol 1, written as part of a Beachwalk Press anthology, was an All Romance eBook bestseller, Amazon bestseller and topped a range of other charts. Two of Imogene's titles have also featured in USA Today's magazine, while Starfire garnered a review in the prestigious Romantic Times magazine.

Imogene is a member of a range of professional organisations, including Romance Writers of Australia, America, and New Zealand. She is also a member of Fantasy, Futuristic and Paranormal Chapter of America, Australian Romance Readers Association, Science Fiction Romance Brigade, the Australian Paranormal, Fantasy and Futuristics, Erotic Writers of Australia, and Queensland Writers Centre.

Over the years, Imogene has mentored a number of beginning authors and continues to engage in these activities, with this work seeing her awarded Senior Cultural Award in 2014 for Gayndah. She still works with beginning and mid-career authors. Imogene has presented and been on panels at a number of events. She is well known on Facebook and Twitter, and keeps a presence on Pinterest, Instagram and Google+.

To learn more about Imogene Nix and new releases, join her newsletter at my Website.

imogenenix.net

**Fiction by Imogene Nix**

**Contemporary**

Tomorrow's Promise

A Bar In Paris

A Sapphire For Karina

**Historical**

Miss Elspeth's Desire

Miss Isabelle's Craving

**Paranormal**

Blood Secrets

The Blood Bride

The Illuminated Witch

The Sorcerer's Touch

Celtic Cupid

Blame The Wine

A Stranger's Embrace

Revenge On Cupid

Dark Souls

The Chocolate Affair

Science Fiction

Warriors Of The Elector

Starline

Starfire

Starburst

Star of Ishtar

Star of the Fleet

Star of Eternity

Webs Series

Tangled Webs

False Webs

Covert Web

Hesparia's Tears

Reunion Trilogy

War's End

The Assassin

Executing Justice

The Plan

Bio-Cybe

**Suspense**

Loving Memories

Shorts

The Shuttle

The Shoe Salon

Airport Tales

**Anthologies**

The Chocolate Affair (Edible Delights II)

Tangled Webs (Sex Love & Aliens)

<u>**Non-Fiction By Imogene Nix**</u>

Self Publishing: Absolute Beginners Guide This Book

You can also find Imogene's books here: Book Depository and All romance Ebook

# *About Suzi Love*

I now live in a sunny part of Australia after spending many years in developing countries in the South Pacific. My greatest loves are traveling, anywhere and everywhere, meeting crazy characters, and visiting the Australian outback.

I adore history, especially the many-layered society of the late Regency to early Victorian eras. My heroes and heroines challenge traditional manners, morals, and occupations, and they might live a privileged life, they also understand the seamier parts of British life.

I'm a member of many writing associations, which I love e.g. Romance Writers of Australia, New Zealand, and America, where I've served in many volunteer positions, Australian Romance Readers Association, Australian Erotic Writers, and The Non-Fiction Association.

I served two years on the board of the American Regency Romance chapter, The Beau Monde, and am also a member of the American history chapter Hearts Through History. I can be found in many Facebook groups talking about books and history and am always busy on Twitter, Google+, Instagram, and my personal favourite, Pinterest, where I have story boards for all my books.

To learn more about Suzi Love and my new releases, join my newsletter at my Website. suzilove.com.

Read about history, books, the Regency Era, and Australia in my Daily Magazine or my Daily Gossip Newspaper , Goodreads and Pinterest.

Tag Line - Making history fun, one year at a time.

I love hearing from my readers so please email me - suzi@SuziLove.com

**<u>Fiction By Suzi Love</u>**

Embracing Scandal Book 1 Scandalous Siblings Series

Scenting Scandal Book 2 Scandalous Siblings Series

December Scandal Book 3 Scandalous Siblings Series

The Viscount's Pleasure House Book 1 Irresistible Aristocrats

Four Times A Virgin Book 2 Irresistible Aristocrats

Petunia and the Pearl Diver

Seven Nights Of Sin

It's In His Kiss

Sexcapades Sizzling Snippets

Loving Lady Katharine Book 3 Irresistible Aristocrats

Love After Waterloo

Pleasure House Ball

Outback Arrival Coming soon

Old Sydney Town Coming soon

## **Non-Fiction By Suzi Love**

History Of Christmases Past Book 1 History Events

Easter In Images Book 2 History Events

Regency Overview Book 1 Regency Life Series

Young Gentleman's Day Book 2 Regency Life Series

Older Gentleman's Day Book 3 Regency Life Series

Young Lady's Day Book 4 Regency Life Series

Older Lady's Day Book 5 Regency Life Series

Self-Publishing: Absolute Beginners Guide - This Book

## *Afterword*

The Regional Arts Development Fund is a partnership between the Queensland Government and the North Burnett Regional Council to support local arts and culture in regional Queensland.

*Notes*

*Notes*

*Notes*

www.ingramcontent.com/pod-product-compliance
Lightning Source LLC
Chambersburg PA
CBHW070630300426
44113CB00010B/1726